Alexander Fanghänel

Scheduling in Wireless Networks with Oblivious Power Assignments

Alexander Fanghänel

Scheduling in Wireless Networks with Oblivious Power Assignments

Analyzing the physical interference model

Südwestdeutscher Verlag für Hochschulschriften

Impressum/Imprint (nur für Deutschland/only for Germany)
Bibliografische Information der Deutschen Nationalbibliothek: Die Deutsche Nationalbibliothek verzeichnet diese Publikation in der Deutschen Nationalbibliografie; detaillierte bibliografische Daten sind im Internet über http://dnb.d-nb.de abrufbar.
Alle in diesem Buch genannten Marken und Produktnamen unterliegen warenzeichen-, marken- oder patentrechtlichem Schutz bzw. sind Warenzeichen oder eingetragene Warenzeichen der jeweiligen Inhaber. Die Wiedergabe von Marken, Produktnamen, Gebrauchsnamen, Handelsnamen, Warenbezeichnungen u.s.w. in diesem Werk berechtigt auch ohne besondere Kennzeichnung nicht zu der Annahme, dass solche Namen im Sinne der Warenzeichen- und Markenschutzgesetzgebung als frei zu betrachten wären und daher von jedermann benutzt werden dürften.

Coverbild: www.ingimage.com

Verlag: Südwestdeutscher Verlag für Hochschulschriften GmbH & Co. KG
Heinrich-Böcking-Str. 6-8, 66121 Saarbrücken, Deutschland
Telefon +49 681 37 20 271-1, Telefax +49 681 37 20 271-0
Email: info@svh-verlag.de

Approved by: Aachen, RWTH, Diss., 2010

Herstellung in Deutschland:
Schaltungsdienst Lange o.H.G., Berlin
Books on Demand GmbH, Norderstedt
Reha GmbH, Saarbrücken
Amazon Distribution GmbH, Leipzig
ISBN: 978-3-8381-3011-8

Imprint (only for USA, GB)
Bibliographic information published by the Deutsche Nationalbibliothek: The Deutsche Nationalbibliothek lists this publication in the Deutsche Nationalbibliografie; detailed bibliographic data are available in the Internet at http://dnb.d-nb.de.
Any brand names and product names mentioned in this book are subject to trademark, brand or patent protection and are trademarks or registered trademarks of their respective holders. The use of brand names, product names, common names, trade names, product descriptions etc. even without a particular marking in this works is in no way to be construed to mean that such names may be regarded as unrestricted in respect of trademark and brand protection legislation and could thus be used by anyone.

Cover image: www.ingimage.com

Publisher: Südwestdeutscher Verlag für Hochschulschriften GmbH & Co. KG
Heinrich-Böcking-Str. 6-8, 66121 Saarbrücken, Germany
Phone +49 681 37 20 271-1, Fax +49 681 37 20 271-0
Email: info@svh-verlag.de

Printed in the U.S.A.
Printed in the U.K. by (see last page)
ISBN: 978-3-8381-3011-8

Copyright © 2011 by the author and Südwestdeutscher Verlag für Hochschulschriften GmbH & Co. KG and licensors
All rights reserved. Saarbrücken 2011

Abstract

In this thesis we analyze scheduling in wireless networks under the physical model. In particular, we ask the following question. Given n communication requests as pairs of nodes from a metric space, how fast can we schedule all of them? We have to assign a schedule slot and a transmission power to each request and need to ensure that during each schedule step the interference at the addressed receivers is not too high. The interference is modeled in terms of the *Signal to Interference Plus Noise Ratio (SINR)* that compares the received signal strength with the sum of all other simultaneously sent signals plus ambient noise. We strive to minimize the schedule length.

We investigate scheduling using *oblivious power assignments* where each request uses a transmission power depending only on the path loss between sender and receiver. The most famous examples of such power assignments are the uniform assignment, where each sender uses the same transmission power, and the linear assignment that uses transmission powers linear in the path loss between the two nodes.

We first present a *measure of interference* that allows us to lower bound the schedule length when using linear or optimal power assignment. Based on this measure of interference we devise distributed scheduling algorithms for the linear power assignment reaching the minimal schedule length up to small factors.

Second, we study the limitations of oblivious power assignments by proving lower bounds for scheduling algorithms using these power assignments. In particular, when only considering the number of nodes in the lower bound, oblivious power assignments cannot yield an approximation ratio asymptotically better than the worst possible performance guarantee.

When modifying the problem to bidirectional communication these lower bounds only hold for some oblivious power assignments, e.g., for uniform and linear power assignment. This motivated us to deeply investigate the

Abstract

bidirectional variant of the problem. Here, in every schedule step the two nodes of a pair can exchange messages in both directions, as long as only one of them acts as a sender at any given time. We present a detailed analysis of bidirectional scheduling using the *square root power assignment* which provides an exponential shorter worst-case schedule than, e. g., the linear or uniform power assignment.

In the last part we raise the question of the capacity of wireless networks in an online setting. To be more specific, requests arrive over time and on arrival of a single request we have to either accept or reject it. The objective is to accept as much requests as possible such that all accepted requests form an SINR feasible set. Not only does our analysis reveal an exponential gap between the performance of deterministic offline and online algorithms, we also present a well-performing randomized algorithm for this problem.

Contents

1 **Introduction**   1
   1.1 Modeling Interference 2
   1.2 The Interference Scheduling Problem 5
       1.2.1 Online Scheduling 6
       1.2.2 Oblivious Power Assignments 7
   1.3 Our Contribution 8
       1.3.1 Analyzing the Linear Power Assignment 8
       1.3.2 Square Root Power and the Bidirectional Model 10
       1.3.3 Online Scheduling 12
   1.4 Related Work 14
       1.4.1 Bibliographical Notes 17

2 **Scheduling with the Linear Power Assignment**   19
   2.1 The Measure of Interference I and Lower Bounds 19
   2.2 Upper Bounds for the Linear Power Assignment 25
   2.3 Extensions for Multi-hop Scheduling and Routing 31
       2.3.1 Multi-hop Scheduling with Fixed Paths 32
       2.3.2 Finding Optimal Paths (Routing) 33
       2.3.3 Consequences for the CLM Problem 34

3 **Oblivious Power Assignments and the Bidirectional Model**   37
   3.1 The Gap of Oblivious Power Schemes 37
   3.2 The Square Root Assignment 42
       3.2.1 Scaling the SINR Threshold 43
       3.2.2 Splitting Pairs 45
       3.2.3 From General Metrics to Trees 47
       3.2.4 From Trees to Stars 48
       3.2.5 Putting the Pieces Together 49

Contents

	3.2.6 Analysis for Star Metrics	50
3.3	A Scheduling Algorithm for the Square Root Power Assignment	61

4 Online Request Scheduling — 69
  4.1 A Simple Algorithm and a Lower Bound 70
  4.2 Competitive Ratios below Δ^d 79
      4.2.1 A Near-Optimal Algorithm for the Square Root Assignment 79
      4.2.2 Multiple Channels 81
      4.2.3 A Randomized Algorithm 82
  4.3 Extensions 83
      4.3.1 Requests with Duration 83
      4.3.2 Doubling Metrics 84

5 Conclusions — 89

Bibliography — 93

Chapter 1

Introduction

The importance and omnipresence of wireless networks raises new challenges for the theoretical computer science community. A deep understanding is necessary not only to analyze throughput and capacity of such networks, but also to develop applicable algorithms that achieve near-optimal performance.

Wireless devices can communicate without a physical connection between them. This useful feature raises new challenges as communication attempts that use the same frequencies interfere with each other. One of the main tasks is carefully balancing the number of simultaneous transmissions since too many transmissions lead to numerous collisions and dropped packets, whereas too few transmissions do not utilize the available spectrum and in this way deteriorate the performance of the network. This highlights the need of developing good scheduling strategies.

In a first step we need to formalize system models that are on the one hand mathematically conceivable, on the other hand reasonable realistic. There are two widely accepted classes of interference models: Graph based (or protocol) models and fading channel models. In graph based models interference is described as a binary property. Usually, two communication links connected by an edge in the graph cannot transmit successfully at the same time. The existence of an edge is often based on the distance between the nodes. Such models have the advantage that graph theoretical results can be directly adapted. Then again, the main criticism is that these models are too simplifying. In fading channel models such as the physical model, which is a widely accepted model in the engineering community, signals fade away with increasing distance from the sender. Thus, interference has a continuous character, which makes the analysis and development of scheduling strategies

1. Introduction

more involved.

Finding good schedules is only one step towards increasing the network utility. A second task is to find suitable transmission powers for the devices as this has great influence on the data rates. First basic analyses assumed that all devices use a specific, fixed transmission power. It turns out that allowing the involved devices to adjust their transmission power can lead to significant improvements.

In this thesis we give a deep insight into such scheduling scenarios with power control. Before giving an outline of our results we present our formal model.

1.1 Modeling Interference

Wireless communication and data transmission are omnipresent. High data rates and low latency are demanded. But the more transmissions take place, the more interference arises, causing a negative effect on these criteria.

Interference has been modeled in various ways. Simple approaches about transmitting data packets in radio networks rely on *graph based vicinity models* of the following flavour. Two nodes in the radio network are connected by an edge in a communication graph if and only if they are in mutual transmission range. Interference is modeled through independence constraints: If a node u transmits a signal to an adjacent node v, then no other node in the vicinity of v, e.g., in the one- or two-hop neighborhood, can transmit. This modeling approach is far from reality. First, the graph theoretical concept of an edge is too simplifying as neither radio signals nor interference end abruptly at a boundary. This can lead to too much interference as the received signals from multiple far away transmissions add up. Second, in reality two close by pairs can transmit simultaneously under the right circumstances. These models are not able to cover such cases.

A more realistic model was presented by Gupta and Kumar [GK98]. This so called *physical model* is well-accepted in the engineering community and gained some interest in recent theoretical work [AD09, ALP09, CKM+07, CKM+08, GHWW09, GOW07, Hal09, MW06, MWZ06]. This model describes interference as a continuous property. It is assumed that the strength of a signal diminishes with the distance from its source. More specifically, let $d(u, v)$ denote the distance between the nodes u and v. We assume the *path*

1.1 Modeling Interference

loss radio propagation model, where a signal sent by node u with power p is received at node v with $p/d(u,v)^\alpha$, where $\alpha \geq 1$ is a parameter of the model, the so-called *path-loss exponent*.[1] Node v can successfully decode this signal if its strength is relatively large in comparison to the strength of other signals received at the same time. This constraint is described in terms of the *Signal to Interference plus Noise Ratio (SINR)* being defined as the ratio between the strength of the signal that shall be received and the sum of the strengths of signals simultaneously sent by other nodes (plus ambient noise). For successfully receiving a signal, it is required that the SINR is at least as large as some hardware-defined threshold $\beta > 0$, the so-called *SINR threshold*.

Recent work compares graph based and physical models, e.g., [MJD08, GH01, MWW06, Mos07, LP10]. They conclude theoretically as well as experimentally that schedules based on the physical model outperform graph based schedules. On the other hand, when restricting certain model parameters from the physical model such as the path-loss exponent or the aspect ratio scheduling in this model reduces up to a constant factor to solutions obtained by graph coloring models [Hal09, LL09, KR10].

In the following, we will illustrate the physical model with a simple but intriguing example also showing the importance of choosing the right power assignment. Suppose there are two pairs of nodes (u_1, v_1) and (u_2, v_2). Two signals shall be sent simultaneously, one from u_1 to v_1 and the other from u_2 to v_2. Suppose the nodes are placed in a nested fashion on a line, that is, the points are located on the line in the order u_1, u_2, v_2, v_1 such that the distance between u_1 and u_2 is 2, the distance between u_2 and v_2 is 1, and the distance between v_2 and v_1 is 2 (cf. Figure 1.1). For simplicity fix $\alpha = 2$ and $\beta = 1$, and neglect the noise.

- At first, let us assume that both u_1 and u_2 send their signal with the same power 1. Then the strength of u_1's signal at node v_1 is $1/25$ while the strength of u_2's signal at the same node is $1/9$. Hence, v_1 cannot decode the signal sent by node u_1 as it is drowned by u_2's signal. That is, the outer pair is blocked by the inner pair when using uniform powers.

- At second, let us assume that signals are sent in a way that the path loss is compensated, that is, both nodes use a strength that is linear

---
[1]Depending on the environment, it is usually assumed that $2 \leq \alpha \leq 5$.

1. Introduction

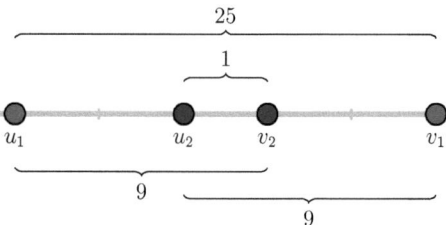

Figure 1.1: Placement of the nodes and the path loss for $\alpha = 2$. Linear and uniform power assignment both need different schedule steps for each of the requests, the square root power assignment can schedule both requests at once.

in the path loss. In particular, u_1 sends at power 25 and u_2 sends at power 1. Now consider the strengths of the signals received at v_2: The strength of u_2's signal is only 1 while the strength of u_1's signal is $25/9$. Thus, the inner pair is blocked by the outer pair when using powers that are chosen linear in the path loss.

- Finally, let us make an attempt setting the powers equal to the square root of the path loss, that is, u_1 uses power 5 and u_2 uses power 1. Now easy calculus shows that, at v_1, the strength of u_1's signal is larger than the strength of u_2's and, at v_2, the strength of u_2's signal is larger than the strength of u_1's. Hence, simultaneous communication between the nested pairs is possible when choosing the right power assignment.

This simple example highlights the power of the physical model. In contrast to graph based models nested pairs of devices can be scheduled simultaneously as long as we choose the right power assignment. Moscibroda et al. [MWW06] created a testbed to show that this effect is not only a theoretical artifact but implementable in a real-world network.

In our previous example the nodes were placed in a one-dimensional metric. In several works, e.g., [CKM+07, AD09], it is assumed that the nodes are placed in the two-dimensional Euclidean space and $\alpha > 2$. In this case the accumulated interference from infinitely many equidistant senders with constant transmission powers is bounded by some constant. A generalization of such a combination of path loss function and distance metric are so-called *fading metrics* [Hal09]. In such fading metrics the path loss coefficient α has to be strictly less than the doubling dimension, that is, the smallest k such that any ball of radius r can be covered by 2^k balls of radius $r/2$.

Most results we are presenting in this thesis are more general, as they hold for general metric spaces and any $\alpha \geq 1$, if not mentioned otherwise.

1.2 The Interference Scheduling Problem

We investigate *interference scheduling problems* like the one in the introducing example. Let V be a set of nodes from a metric space and let $d(u,v)$ denote the distance between two nodes $u, v \in V$. Let the *aspect ratio* $\Delta = \max_{u,v}\{d(u,v)\}/\min_{u,v}\{d(u,v)\}$ denote the ratio between the longest and the shortest distance between any two nodes. W.l.o.g. let the distances be scaled such that $\min_{u,v}\{d(u,v)\} = 1$ and $\max_{u,v}\{d(u,v)\} = \Delta$.

One is given a set $\mathcal{R}$ of n requests each consisting of a pair $(u_i, v_i) \in V^2$, where u_i is the source and v_i is the destination of the signal from the i-th communication request. For every $i \in [n] := \{1, \ldots, n\}$ we need to specify a *power level* $p_i > 0$ and a *color* $c_i \in [k]$ such that the *latency*, i.e., the number of colors k, is minimized and the request pairs in each color class satisfy the following *SINR constraint*:

$$\frac{p_i}{d(u_i, v_i)^\alpha} \geq \beta \left(\sum_{\substack{j \in [n]\setminus\{i\} \\ c_j = c_i}} \frac{p_j}{d(u_j, v_i)^\alpha} + N \right). \qquad (1.1)$$

In this expression α is the *path loss exponent* that characterizes the decay of a signal over a distance. The exact value of α depends on external conditions such as obstacles, reflections and humidity. Several measurements for indoor and outdoor path loss exponents can be found in [Rap01], where α ranges from 1.6 to 6. Our analyses hold for $\alpha \geq 1$, unless stated otherwise. The hardware-dependent constant β is the so-called *SINR threshold*. We assume $\beta > 0$. Finally, the constant N expresses *ambient noise*.

The SINR constraint (Equation 1.1) is the central condition for successful communication in the physical model. It characterizes the strength at v_i of the signal emitted by u_i compared to *ambient noise* and the *interference* from

1. Introduction

signals of all other senders that are assigned the same color (corresponding to time slots or non-interfering channels).

The most common communication protocols used in practice rely on bidirectional point-to-point communication. This is reflected by the following variant of the physical model in which requests are undirected, that is, each of the two nodes of a request acts both as sender and receiver. In this bidirectional problem variant the SINR-constraint is adapted as follows. For all requests $i \in [n]$ and each $w \in \{u_i, v_i\}$, it must hold

$$\frac{p_i}{d(u_i, v_i)^\alpha} \geq \beta \left(\sum_{\substack{j \in [n] \setminus \{i\} \\ c_j = c_i}} \frac{p_j}{\min\{d(u_j, w)^\alpha, d(v_j, w)^\alpha\}} + N \right). \quad (1.2)$$

Here the distance between two nodes from different request pairs i and j is always the shortest distance between those pairs, that is, it equals $\min\{d(u_i, u_j), d(u_i, v_j), d(v_i, v_j), d(u_j, v_i)\}$. In every request set that fulfills the bidirectional SINR condition the two nodes of a request can exchange messages in both directions, as long as only one of them acts as sender at any given time. An alternative way of understanding this model is the following. Each request pair i induces two *directed* links (u_i, v_i) and (v_i, u_i) and each solution is restricted to use the same transmission power for both links.

1.2.1 Online Scheduling

In this section we introduce an online variant of the interference scheduling problem. We receive an unknown number of n communication requests sequentially over time. As in the offline model, each request $i \in [n]$ consists of a point pair from a metric space V with a distance function $d(u, v)$ for $u, v \in V$. Further, each request pair i comes with a parameter t_i, which denotes the duration of the request. We denote by $\Gamma = (\max_i t_i)/(\min_i t_i)$, where w.l.o.g. we let $\min_i t_i = 1$ and $\max_i t_i = \Gamma$.

Requests arrive sequentially over time. The goal is to accept the maximum number of requests that can successfully communicate simultaneously, that is, to maximize the *capacity*. For each request an online algorithm must make a decision whether to accept the request or not. For an accepted request i it needs to set a *power level* p_i and a *channel* $k_i \in \{1 \ldots, k\}$ for the sender u_i to emit a signal. The algorithm maintains the sets $S_1, \ldots, S_k$ of accepted

1.2 The Interference Scheduling Problem

requests on the corresponding channels. Decisions on acceptance, power levels, and channels of a request cannot be revoked later on. If a request is accepted, the algorithm must ensure that it remains successful throughout its duration. The criterion of "successful" for an accepted directed request i is the SINR constraint (Equation 1.1) modified for the available channels:

$$\frac{p_i}{d(u_i, v_i)^\alpha} \geq \beta \left(\sum_{\substack{j \in S_{k_i} \\ j \neq i}} \frac{p_j}{d(u_j, v_i)^\alpha} + N_{k_i} \right) . \tag{1.3}$$

An online algorithm has to ensure that Equation 1.3 is satisfied for all $i \in S = S_1 \cup \ldots \cup S_k$ throughout. The adaption for the bidirectional model is straight forward and not stated explicitly. When we try to find maximum feasible subsets of requests we will refer to this as *capacity maximization problems*.

For the analysis of our online algorithms we make use of the following definitions. Let $A(\omega)$ denote the number of request pairs an online algorithm A accepts, and let $\text{OPT}(\omega)$ denote the number of requests in an optimal offline solution on an input sequence ω. An online algorithm is *c-competitive* (or "yields competitive ratio c") if there exists a constant a, such that for every input ω

$$A(\omega) \geq (\text{OPT}(\omega)/c) + a .$$

We call algorithm A *strictly c*-competitive if it is *c*-competitive with $a = 0$. All algorithms we present in Chapter 4 are strictly competitive. For the lower bounds we do not need to rely on strictness.

1.2.2 Oblivious Power Assignments

The presented interference scheduling problems consist of two correlated subproblems: the *power assignment* and the *coloring* (for schedule minimization) or *selection* (for capacity maximization). In this thesis we shed light on scheduling with distance-based power assignments, as they are locally computable independent of other requests. This locality allows an immediate implementation in a distributed setting.

By far most literature focuses on scheduling with *uniform power assignment*, in which all pairs send at the same power, i.e., $p_i = 1$ for each request

1. Introduction

i (see, e.g., [GK98, HM04, SR98]). These power assignments are motivated by devices without power control which is a common characteristic for sensor network devices [ALPP09]. In other studies, the *linear power assignment* is considered, in which the power level for a pair is chosen proportional to the path loss, i.e. $p_i = d(u_i, v_i)^\alpha$, (e.g., [BM02, CKM+07, WNE02]). The linear power assignment has the advantage of being energy-efficient as the minimal transmission power required to transmit along a distance d is $\Theta(d^\alpha)$. Furthermore, in the introducing example we have seen that *square root* (or *mean*) assignments which set powers proportional to the square root of the path loss ($p_i = \sqrt{d(u_i, v_i)^\alpha}$) might be an interesting alternative, as they – in contrast to linear and uniform power assignments – allow to schedule nested pairs of requests.

In this thesis we focus on such distance-based power assignments because of their simplicity and locality, which is a striking conceptual advantage in distributed wireless systems. A *distance-based* (or *oblivious*) power assignment p is given by $p_i = \phi(d(u_i, v_i))$ with a function $\phi : [1, \Delta] \to (0, \infty)$. For uniqueness we assume ϕ is always scaled such that $\phi(1) = 1$. A slightly more narrow class is the class of *polynomial* assignments of the form $\phi(d(u_i, v_i)) = d(u_i, v_i)^{r\alpha}$ with parameter $r \in \mathbb{R}$. Both, the class of oblivious and the class of polynomial assignments include uniform, linear and square root assignments.

1.3 Our Contribution

1.3.1 Analyzing the Linear Power Assignment

In Chapter 2 we focus on the linear power assignments, i.e., for a request pair (u_i, v_i) the power is $p_i = d(u_i, v_i)^\alpha$ and, hence, linear in fading. Linear power schemes also have been considered in [BM02, CKM+07, WNE02]. Our analysis will show that one loses only a factor of order $\log \Delta$ due to restricting to this power scheme. Let us remark that the dependence on the aspect ratio Δ cannot be avoided using a linear power assignment which, without taking into account other parameters than n, cannot achieve an approximation ratio better than $\Omega(n)$ (see Section 3.1).

We introduce an instance-based measure of interference that enables us to estimate the optimal schedule length of any set of requests within small factors.

1.3 Our Contribution

Definition 1.3.1 (Measure of Interference). *Let $\mathcal{R} \subseteq V \times V$ be a set of requests. For $w \in V$ define*

$$I_w(\mathcal{R}) = \sum_{(u,v) \in \mathcal{R}} \min\left\{1, \frac{d(u,v)^\alpha}{d(u,w)^\alpha}\right\} .$$

Using this we define the measure of interference induced by the requests $\mathcal{R}$:

$$I = I(\mathcal{R}) = \max_{w \in V} I_w(\mathcal{R}) .$$

In Chapter 2 we present upper and lower bounds for the optimal schedule length in terms of I, i.e., we bound the number of steps needed for scheduling $\mathcal{R}$. When the requests are placed in any metric space and the power assignment of the optimal solution is not restricted at all, we can prove the following lower bound.

Theorem 1.3.2. *For a set of requests, every schedule using an arbitrary power assignment has length at least $\Omega\left(I/\log \Delta \cdot \log n\right)$.*

This bound improves to $\Omega(I/\log \Delta)$, when restricting to the two-dimensional Euclidean space and assuming $\alpha > 2$. Alternatively, when restricting to linear power assignments and assuming general metrics, this bound improves even to $\Omega(I)$. We complement these lower bounds with two efficient algorithms. The first, very basic algorithm computes a schedule for linear power assignments using only $\mathcal{O}(I \cdot \log n)$ steps. For a slightly more involved algorithm we derive the following upper bound.

Theorem 1.3.3. *For any instance there exists a schedule under the linear power assignment of length at most $\mathcal{O}(I + \log^2 n)$ steps whp[2].*

This results in a constant-factor approximation of the optimal schedule under linear power assignments for *dense* instances, i.e., if $I \geq \log^2 n$. To the best of our knowledge, this result is so far the only constant-factor approximation for the scheduling problem in the physical model. Combining this upper bound for linear power assignments with the lower bound for general power assignments and the two-dimensional Euclidean space shows that the price for using linear, in other words, energy-efficient power assignments is of order $\mathcal{O}(\log \Delta)$.

---

[2] with high probability: with probability $1 - n^{-c}$ for any constant $c > 0$

1. Introduction

We further extend our results towards multi-hop scheduling and routing. In the multi-hop scheduling problem, a request is defined by a sequence of pairs, so-called *paths*, rather than a single pair of nodes. Along each of these paths, one should forward a message from the first to the last node on the path. Let D denote the maximum number of hops on each of these paths, the so-called *dilation*. Generalizing, the lower bounds from the single-hop to the multi-hop problem, shows that one needs at least $\Omega(I/_{\log \Delta \log n} + D)$ steps, for general power assignments, $\Omega(I/_{\log \Delta} + D)$ for the Euclidean space, and $\Omega(I + D)$ steps, for linear power assignments. We show how to extend our second algorithm for the single-hop scheduling to the multi-hop case, where it produces a schedule of at most $\mathcal{O}(I + D \cdot \log^2 n)$ steps.

These results for multi-hop scheduling remind of the $\mathcal{O}(\text{congestion} + \text{dilation})$-type results that have been shown previously for routing in wired networks, see, e. g., [adHV95, LMR94, LMRR94, ST97]. In fact, this previous work was the inspiration to search for an instance-based density measure that allows to derive lower bounds for the scheduling complexity in wireless networks like the congestion in wired networks. At this point, let us remark that, unlike the congestion, our interference measure I does not trivially give a lower bound on the number of steps needed for scheduling a set of requests but it requires a careful analysis as also the upper bound does.

We then show how to extend our result to combined multi-hop routing and scheduling. Now requests are again defined by pairs of nodes. The problem is to find source-destination paths for all requests and to compute a power assignment and a schedule delivering all packets using as few steps as possible. Combining our multi-hop scheduling algorithm with a linear programming approach for computing paths that minimize the term $\max\{I, D\}$ gives an $\mathcal{O}(\log \Delta \log^3 n)$-approximation for the combined routing and scheduling problem in general metrics. In the two-dimensional Euclidean space the approximation factor is $\mathcal{O}(\log \Delta \log^2 n)$. This generalizes the results from Chafekar et al. [CKM+07] (cf. Section 1.4) towards general metrics and improves on their approximation factors.

1.3.2 Square Root Power and the Bidirectional Model

In Chapter 3 we turn our focus on oblivious power assignments. We study the question whether those power assignments are efficient with respect to the schedule length (or, equivalently, number of colors) they require in com-

1.3 Our Contribution

parison to an optimal schedule. Our answer to this question is different depending on whether one considers the directed or bidirectional version of the problem.

For the directed scheduling problem we prove the following.

Theorem 1.3.4. *For any oblivious power assignment p there exists a family of instances with n directed communication requests needing $\Omega(n)$ schedule steps when using p, but only a constant number of steps when using an optimal power assignment.*

Thus, when considering only the size of the input, oblivious power assignments cannot yield approximation ratios better than n for the directed interference scheduling problem, which corresponds to the worst possible performance guarantee. As a consequence, the dependence on the aspect ratio Δ cannot be avoided when considering oblivious power assignments on directed request sets. We also show that, when taking the aspect ratio into account, there is a gap of $\Omega(\sqrt{\log \log \Delta})$ between oblivious and non-oblivious power schemes.

The negative results for the directed variant are shown by specifying families of request pairs on the line. That is, these results hold already for the one-dimensional Euclidean space. In contrast, the following positive result about the bidirectional variant holds for request pairs from every metric space.

Theorem 1.3.5. *For any set of n bidirectional requests, the square root power assignment admits a schedule that is at most $\mathrm{polylog}(n)$ times longer than an optimal schedule.*

The introductory example with the nested request pairs on the line already gave an intuition what is the secret behind the square root power assignment. Our analysis shows that this kind of balancing effect does not only exist for the line but it is present in any metric space.

The proof for the existence of the schedule in the bidirectional case relies on simulating general metrics by tree metrics and then, as a next step, decomposing tree metrics into star metrics in a hierarchical manner. Our existence proof is non-constructive. We make our result constructive by additionally giving an efficient approximation algorithm for the scheduling problem under the square root assignment. This way, we obtain the first polynomial time

1. Introduction

algorithm with approximation ratio polylog(n) for interference scheduling in the physical model.

These motivating results for the bidirectional model were first presented in [FKRV09] and triggered the research on the square root power assignment, see, e. g., [Hal09, HM10].

1.3.3 Online Scheduling

The drawback of all previous treatments of the physical model is that they neglect the dynamic structure of this problem. In Chapter 4 we focus on this aspect. In particular, we analyze *capacity maximization* in an online setting, that is, we aim to maximize the number of accepted requests rather than scheduling all requests. The offline version of this problem received a lot of attention, e. g., [AD09, GHWW09].

In the online version of this problem requests arrive over time one by one. An online algorithm has to decide whether to accept an incoming request or not and assign the accepted requests a transmission power. Decisions about acceptance as well as power assignments cannot be revoked later on.

Our first contribution are lower bounds for deterministic online algorithms choosing requests for a single channel. We show the following lower bound for deterministic online algorithms.

Theorem 1.3.6. *Every deterministic online algorithm using a polynomial power assignment has a competitive ratio of* $\Omega\left(\Gamma \cdot \Delta^{d \cdot \max\{r, 1-r\}}\right)$. *Every deterministic online algorithm is* $\Omega\left(\Gamma \cdot \Delta^{d/2}\right)$-*competitive*

- *using arbitrary power assignments in the case of bidirectional requests and*

- *using distance-based power assignments in the case of only directed requests.*

For uniform and linear power assignments, this result yields a lower bound of $\Omega\left(\Gamma \cdot \Delta^{d}\right)$; for the square root power assignment, we get lower bound of $\Omega\left(\Gamma \cdot \Delta^{d/2}\right)$. In fact, we can show that the $\Omega\left(\Gamma \cdot \Delta^{d/2}\right)$ lower bound on the competitive ratio is not restricted to polynomial power assignments: In the case of directed requests, this bound holds for any distance-based power assignment and, in the case of bidirectional requests, the same bound holds even for general power assignments.

1.3 Our Contribution

Our lower bounds reveal an exponential gap between the approximation guarantees achievable by deterministic online and offline algorithms. The main difficulty of the online scenario turns out to be that requests cannot be ordered by length. This has been a crucial ingredient to all existing deterministic offline algorithms with polylogarithmic approximation guarantee [AD09, GHWW09, Hal09].

Our second contribution is a deterministic online algorithm for a single channel that almost matches the lower bounds. All following results hold for directed and bidirectional requests. Algorithm SAFE-DISTANCE works for polynomial power assignments with $r \in [0, 1]$. For uniform and linear power assignments, it achieves a competitive ratio of $\mathcal{O}\left(\Gamma \cdot \Delta^d\right)$. For the square root power assignment, we extend the basic idea and obtain algorithm MULTI-CLASS SAFE-DISTANCE, which achieves the following near-optimal competitive ratio.

Theorem 1.3.7. *For any constant $\varepsilon > 0$,* MULTI-CLASS SAFE-DISTANCE *is $\mathcal{O}\left(\Gamma \cdot \Delta^{d/2+\varepsilon}\right)$-competitive for a single channel using the square root power assignment.*

Let us explicitly point out that these competitive ratios compare the performance of online algorithms with polynomial power assignments to optimal offline algorithms with general power assignments. Combining the upper bound for the square root power assignment with the lower bounds above shows that this power assignment achieves nearly the best possible competitive ratio among all (distance-based) power assignments (in case of directed requests) and is superior to any other polynomial power assignment.

Our third contribution is an illustration of the power of multiple channels for deterministic online algorithms. We generalize algorithm MULTI-CLASS SAFE-DISTANCE and its analysis from 1 to k channels and achieve an exponential reduction in the competitive ratio. We prove that algorithm MULTI-CLASS SAFE-DISTANCE using $k = k' \cdot k''$ channels is only $\mathcal{O}\left(k \cdot \Gamma^{1/k'} \cdot \Delta^{(d/2k'')+\varepsilon}\right)$-competitive. In particular, with just a logarithmic number of channels we obtain a deterministic algorithm with logarithmic competitive ratio. This algorithm is only constant-competitive against an optimum solution that uses only one channel. By randomly choosing a channel, we thus obtain a randomized algorithm RANDOM SAFE-DISTANCE for a single channel that beats the deterministic lower bounds.

1. Introduction

	Channels	Uniform/Linear	Square root
Determ.	1	$\Theta\left(\Gamma \cdot \Delta^d\right)$	$\mathcal{O}\left(\Gamma \cdot \Delta^{d/2+\varepsilon}\right)$ $\Omega\left(\Gamma \cdot \Delta^{d/2}\right)$
	k	$\mathcal{O}\left(k \cdot \Gamma^{1/k_1} \cdot \Delta^{d/k_2}\right)$	$\mathcal{O}\left(k \cdot \Gamma^{1/k_1} \cdot \Delta^{(d/2k_2)+\varepsilon}\right)$
Random.	1	$\Theta(\log \Gamma \cdot \log \Delta)$	$\mathcal{O}(\log \Gamma \cdot \log \Delta)$ $\Omega(\log \log \Gamma \cdot \log \log \Delta)$
	k		$\mathcal{O}(\log \Gamma \cdot \log \Delta)$

Table 1.1: Main results of Chapter 4.

Corollary 1.3.8. RANDOM SAFE-DISTANCE *is* $\mathcal{O}(\log \Gamma \cdot \log \Delta)$-*competitive for any polynomial power assignment.*

Finally, we show the robustness of our results by extending all upper bounds from Euclidean to doubling metrics. This allows to introduce features such as obstacles in our model, which locally disturb Euclidean distances but do not affect the global structure of the metric.

In Table 1.1 we give a structured summary of the results presented in Chapter 4.

1.4 Related Work

The first theoretical studies about interference scheduling in the physical model focus on topologies generated by placing nodes randomly in two-dimensional Euclidean space, see, e.g., [BL03, GK00, KT03].

Studying the capacity of wireless networks with respect to arbitrary topologies has been initiated by Moscibroda and Wattenhofer [MW06]. They present the first worst-case analysis of the interference scheduling problem. However, they do not handle general request sets but only specific kinds of sets. In particular, they study the question of how many time slots are needed to schedule a set of communication requests ensuring strong connectivity among n points placed arbitrarily in two-dimensional Euclidean space. On the one hand, they prove that there are configurations requiring $\Omega(n)$ time slots using either uniform or linear power assignments, when not taking other

1.4 Related Work

parameters, like the aspect ratio Δ, into account. On the other hand, they show that $\mathcal{O}(\log^4 n)$ time slots are sufficient to ensure strong connectivity when choosing the right power assignment.

After this seminal work several authors considered versions of the scheduling problem independently. One wide branch of research analyses scheduling for uniform power assignments.

The best known result for uniform power assignments is achieved by Goussevskaia et al. in [GHWW09, Gou09]. They present the first topology-independent algorithm that achieves an $\mathcal{O}(1)$ approximation guarantee with respect to the number of requests that can be scheduled simultaneously when restricting to uniform power assignments. Repeatedly applying this result to a set of request yields an $\mathcal{O}(\log n)$ approximation for the scheduling problem using uniform power. Halldórsson and Wattenhofer [HW09] introduce the *affectance*, a function closely related to our measure of interference (cf. Definition 1.3.1). They claim that their affectance-based algorithm yields a constant-factor approximation for scheduling with uniform powers. Unfortunately, due to a faulty claim in [HW09] the question whether the scheduling problem using uniform powers is $\mathcal{O}(1)$-approximable still remains open.

Kesselheim and Vöcking [KV10] generalize the idea of an interference measure for a broader class of monotone power assignments, including uniform and square root power assignment. For a fixed power assignment, they introduce the *maximum average affectance* $\bar{A}$ and show that it is at most an $\mathcal{O}(\log n)$ factor away from the optimal schedule length. They first present a basic algorithm, that uses transmission probabilities depending on $\bar{A}$ for each request. With an *exponential backoff* and a nontrivial way of sending *acknowledgments* they obtain a fully decentralized algorithm which yields an $\mathcal{O}(\log^2 n)$ approximation factor.

Goussevskaia et al. [GMW08] examine the local broadcasting problem where any node in the network intends to transmit a packet to all nodes within its so-called *local broadcasting range*. They describe two distributed algorithms which have a polylogarithmic approximation factor.

In [ALPP09] Avin et al. study the connectivity problem for wireless grid networks under uniform power. They show that the number of colors needed for strong connectivity is constant in two-dimensional grids if $\alpha > 2$.

The work of Avin et al. [AEK+09] gives an insight, which possibilities and restrictions are caused by uniform powers. They study properties of SINR diagrams, i.e., graphs that depict *reception regions* for a given instance under

1. Introduction

uniform power assignment. They show that every reception region is convex (for $\alpha > 0$ and $\beta \geq 1$) and fat (for $\alpha = 2$ and $\beta > 1$).

In [ALP09] Avin et al. study the capacity maximization problem for uniform power with *bounded resources*. On the one hand they bound the length L of the network for one-dimensional networks. Here they show constructively that when changing the power assignment from optimal to uniform power one loses at least a factor of $\Omega(\log L)$, which matches with the upper bound of an example from [MOW07]. On the other hand they allow only power levels in $[1, p_{\max}]$ and prove that scheduling with uniform powers yields a schedule of length $\Theta(n/\log p_{\max})$. They show that the usual worst-case examples that grow exponentially will rarely occur in practical, resource-bounded instances. This motivates solving such problems for the simpler uniform power model and then get rid of the logarithmic factor for general powers.

Andrews and Dinitz [AD09] consider the capacity maximization problem from a game theoretic point of view and present an $\mathcal{O}(\log \Delta)$ approximation. They further show that it is NP-hard to find a maximal feasible subset of requests. This work was extended by Dinitz in [Din10] towards a distributed setting by using a no-regret algorithm.

The results from [FKRV09] (which we will present in this thesis) bring focus to the square root power assignment and show that in the bidirectional model a schedule at most $\mathcal{O}(\text{polylog}\, n)$ longer than a schedule using optimal powers exists. This result was improved by Halldórsson [Hal09] to a factor of $\mathcal{O}(\log n)$ in fading metrics. Further he proves that the optimal schedule length is at most an $\mathcal{O}(\log \log \Delta \cdot \log n)$ factor worse than one using the optimal power assignment. Recently, Halldórsson and Mitra [HM10] further improve on these results. For the capacity maximization problem, they present an $\mathcal{O}(1)$-approximation algorithm for any length monotone, sublinear power assignment in general metrics. They use this algorithm to prove that scheduling in the bidirectional model is bounded by $\mathcal{O}(\log n)$ in general metrics. This upper bound matches asymptotically with their lower bound of $\Omega(\log n)$ for bidirectional scheduling with oblivious power assignments. Their result underlines the strength of the square root power assignment, as this transmission power is essentially the best possible for the scheduling problem in the bidirectional setting.

Other work uses some more complicated, non-oblivious power assignments. Moscibroda et al. [MWZ06] extend the results from [MW06] to arbitrary demands. They introduce a certain interference measure I_{in} and present

1.4 Related Work

an $\mathcal{O}(\log^2 n \cdot I_{\text{in}})$ algorithm. This result enables them to improve the bound for strong connectivity from $\mathcal{O}(\log^4 n)$ to $\mathcal{O}(\log^3 n)$. Unfortunately, I_{in} is no lower bound for the optimal schedule length. Thus, it does not give any approximation guarantee for general request sets since there is no comparison between I_{in} and the optimal schedule length.

Chafekar et al. [CKM+07] study the combined routing and multi-hop version of the interference scheduling problem. It is crucial for their analysis to deal with two-dimensional Euclidean instances and $\alpha > 2$. This allows to use graph coloring in a way similar to the approaches used in the graph theoretical vicinity models. In their analysis the considered power assignment is restricted, that is, it is assumed that power levels must be chosen from a specified interval $[1, p_{\max}]$. It yields a schedule using $\mathcal{O}(\text{opt}' \cdot \log^2 n \log \Delta \log^2 p_{\max})$ time slots where opt' denotes the minimal number of time slots needed for a schedule with slightly smaller power range $[1, (1-\epsilon)p_{\max}]$.

Another branch of research focuses on power control. First power control algorithms had a heuristic nature. In [EE04], ElBatt and Ephremides propose a power control algorithm with the following idea. They start with an arbitrary power assignment and modify the power for each pair in a given iteration step to overcome the noise plus interference from the previous step. This iteration converges to the optimal assignment, as long as a feasible power assignment exists. To derive a scheduling algorithm from such a power control approach, one selects a set of requests with guaranteed existence of a fixed point for the power control mechanism. Moscibroda et al. [MOW07] discussed these approaches and proved a bad worst-case performance for a number of heuristics.

The long open question of approximating optimal powers in the physical model was recently addressed by Kesselheim [Kes10]. He presents an algorithm that yields a constant-factor approximation for capacity maximization in fading metrics. The same algorithm achieves a bound of $\mathcal{O}(\log n)$ in general metrics.

1.4.1 Bibliographical Notes

Most of the results presented in this thesis have been published as joint work at various conferences. The results regarding the linear power assignment presented in Chapter 2 appeared in [FKV09]. The in-depth analysis of bidirectional scheduling in the physical model using square root power

1. Introduction

(see Chapter 3) were sketched in [FKRV09]. The online model we discuss in Chapter 4 was first analyzed in [FGHV10].

Chapter 2
Scheduling with the Linear Power Assignment

In this chapter we focus on the interference scheduling problem with the *linear power assignment*, i.e., the power for a request pair (u_i, v_i) is proportional to $d(u_i, v_i)^\alpha$ and, hence, linear in the path loss. The linear power assignment has the advantage of being energy efficient as the minimal transmission power required to transmit along a distance $d(u_i, v_i)$ is proportional to $d(u_i, v_i)^\alpha$.

In Section 2.1 we present our measure of interference I, which allows us to lower bound the schedule for general metrics using the linear power assignment by $\Omega(I)$. If we allow any power assignment, the schedule length can be bounded by $\Omega(I/\log \Delta \log n)$. For $\alpha > 2$, embedding the instance in the Euclidean space improves this bound to $\mathcal{O}(I/\log \Delta)$.

These results are complemented in Section 2.2 by a simple and efficient algorithm computing a schedule using $\mathcal{O}(I \cdot \log n)$ steps. A more sophisticated algorithm computes a schedule using $\mathcal{O}(I + \log^2 n)$ steps. This gives a constant-factor approximation of the optimal schedule using the linear power assignment for dense instances, i.e., if $I \geq \log^2 n$. These results are extended to multi-hop scheduling in Section 2.3.

2.1 The Measure of Interference I and Lower Bounds

We first present an instance-based *measure of interference I*. This allows us to lower bound the number of steps needed for scheduling a request set $\mathcal{R}$ in

2. Scheduling with the Linear Power Assignment

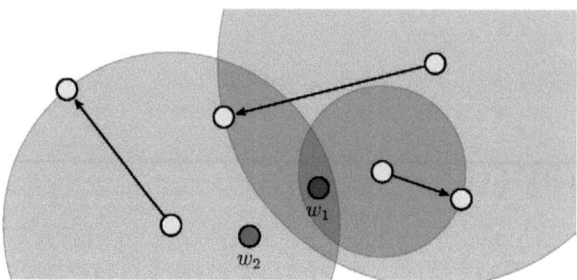

Figure 2.1: An example for the measure of interference with three requests. Gray circles mark the areas where the interference from a sender is at least 1. For the red node I_{w_2} is 1 plus the interference from the two rightmost senders (each less than 1). The interference is maximal at the blue node w_1, i.e., $I_{w_1} = 3$, so the measure of interference I for this instance is $I = 3$.

terms of I.

Definition 2.1.1 (Measure of Interference). *Let $\mathcal{R} \subseteq V \times V$ be a set of requests. For $w \in V$ define*

$$I_w(\mathcal{R}) = \sum_{(u,v)\in\mathcal{R}} \min\left\{1, \frac{d(u,v)^\alpha}{d(u,w)^\alpha}\right\} .$$

Using this function we define the measure of interference induced by the requests in $\mathcal{R}$:

$$I = I(\mathcal{R}) = \max_{w\in V} I_w(\mathcal{R}) .$$

Figure 2.1 illustrates an example of the measure of interference. The instance depicted there consists of three requests, the gray circles mark areas where the interference of the corresponding sender is at least 1 while transmitting and, thus, the minimum in the measure of interference evaluates to 1. The measure of interference at w_2 is 1 plus the interference from the two rightmost senders (each less than 1, depending on the exact value of α). At w_1 it is $I_{w_1} = 3$, which is at the same time the measure of interference I for the whole instance.

Observe that I is subadditive, i.e., for $\mathcal{R} = \mathcal{R}_1 \cup \mathcal{R}_2$ it holds

$$I(\mathcal{R}) = \max_{w\in V} I_w(\mathcal{R}) \leq \max_{w\in V} \{I_w(\mathcal{R}_1) + I_w(\mathcal{R}_2)\}$$

2.1 The Measure of Interference I and Lower Bounds

$$\leq \max_{w\in V} I_w(\mathcal{R}_1) + \max_{w\in V} I_w(\mathcal{R}_2) = I(\mathcal{R}_1) + I(\mathcal{R}_2) \ .$$

We first present a lower bound comparing the measure of interference with the optimal schedule using the linear power assignment in general metrics.

Theorem 2.1.2. *For a set of requests, every schedule using the linear power assignment has length at least $\Omega(I)$.*

Proof. Assume there is a schedule of length T when using the linear power assignment. Then there exist sets of requests $\mathcal{R}_1, \ldots, \mathcal{R}_T$ each of which satisfies the SINR constraint for this power assignment. As I is subadditive we have $I\left(\bigcup_{t=1}^T \mathcal{R}_t\right) \leq \sum_{t=1}^T I(\mathcal{R}_t)$. Thus it suffices to show that $I(\mathcal{R}_t) = \mathcal{O}(1)$ for every $t \in \{1, \ldots, T\}$, as this implies $T = \Omega(I)$.

Let $\mathcal{R}_t = \{(u_1, v_1), \ldots, (u_{\bar{n}}, v_{\bar{n}})\}$ and let $w \in V$. Furthermore, let v_j be the receiver from $\mathcal{R}_t$ that is closest to w, i.e., $j \in \arg\min_{i \in [\bar{n}]} d(v_i, w)$. Possibly it holds that $w = v_j$.

We distinguish between two kinds of requests. We define a set U of indices of requests whose senders u_i lie within a distance of at most $\frac{1}{2} d(v_j, w)$ from w, i.e., $U = \{i \in [\bar{n}] \mid d(u_i, w) \leq \frac{1}{2} d(v_j, w)\}$. First we upper bound $I_w(\mathcal{R}_t \setminus U)$. For all $i \in [\bar{n}] \setminus U$ it holds that

$$d(u_i, v_j) \leq d(u_i, w) + d(w, v_j) \leq d(u_i, w) + 2d(u_i, w) = 3d(u_i, w)$$

by applying triangle inequality and the definition of U. Thus, it follows

$$I_w(\mathcal{R}_t \setminus U) \leq \sum_{\substack{i \in [\bar{n}] \setminus U \\ i \neq j}} \frac{d(u_i, v_i)^\alpha}{d(u_i, w)^\alpha} \leq \sum_{\substack{i \in [\bar{n}] \setminus U \\ i \neq j}} \frac{d(u_i, v_i)^\alpha}{\frac{1}{3^\alpha} d(u_i, v_j)^\alpha} \leq \frac{3^\alpha}{\beta} \ .$$

Next we bound $I_w(U)$. Using the triangle inequality we can conclude for all $i \in U$

$$d(u_i, v_j) \leq d(u_i, w) + d(w, v_j) \leq \frac{3}{2} d(v_j, w) \ . \quad (2.1)$$

In addition, it holds

$$d(v_j, w) \leq d(v_i, w) \leq d(v_i, u_i) + d(u_i, w) \leq d(v_i, u_i) + \frac{1}{2} d(v_j, w) \ .$$

Here the first inequality is true since v_j is the closest receiver to w, the second step holds by triangle inequality and the third step follows from the definition

21

2. Scheduling with the Linear Power Assignment

of U. This implies
$$d(v_j, w) \leq 2d(u_i, v_i) \ . \tag{2.2}$$
Combining Equation 2.1 and Equation 2.2 we get $d(u_i, v_j) \leq 3d(u_i, v_i)$. Thus it follows
$$|U \setminus \{j\}| = \sum_{\substack{i \in U \\ i \neq j}} \frac{d(u_i, v_i)^\alpha}{d(u_i, v_i)^\alpha} \leq \sum_{\substack{i \in U \\ i \neq j}} \frac{d(u_i, v_i)^\alpha}{\frac{1}{3^\alpha} d(u_i, v_j)^\alpha} \leq \frac{3^\alpha}{\beta} \ ,$$
and, hence,
$$I_w(U) = \sum_{i \in U} \min\left\{1, \frac{d(u_i, v_i)^\alpha}{d(u_i, w)^\alpha}\right\} \leq \frac{3^\alpha}{\beta} + 1 \ .$$
In conclusion, with the bounds for $I_w(U)$ and $I_w(\mathcal{R}_t \setminus U)$ we get
$$I_w(\mathcal{R}_t) \leq I_w(U) + I_w(\mathcal{R}_t \setminus U) = \frac{2 \cdot 3^\alpha}{\beta} + 1 = \mathcal{O}(1) \ .$$

□

Next we present a lower bound on the optimal schedule length using an optimal power assignment in general metrics.

Theorem 2.1.3. *For a set of requests, every schedule using an arbitrary power assignment has length at least* $\Omega\left(1/\log \Delta \cdot \log n\right)$.

Proof. We use a similar technique as in the proof of Theorem 2.1.2. However, the main challenge here is to deal with an unknown power assignment. Since there is a schedule of length T in this power assignment, there exist sets of requests $\mathcal{R}_1, \ldots, \mathcal{R}_T$ each of which satisfies the SINR constraint for this power assignment. We divide such a set $\mathcal{R}_t$ into $\log \Delta$ classes $C_{t,j} = \{(u, v) \in \mathcal{R}_t \mid 2^{j-1} \leq d(u, v) < 2^j\}$. Again, by using the subadditivity of I, it suffices to show that $I(C_{t,j}) = \mathcal{O}(\log n)$ for such a class. Fix $C_{t,j}$ and let $C_{t,j} = \{(u_1, v_1), \ldots, (u_{\bar{n}}, v_{\bar{n}})\}$. Further, for notational simplicity we write $L = 2^{j-1}$.

We can bound the number of requests whose senders are located around a node within a distance of at most ℓ.

Lemma 2.1.4. *For all* $w \in V$ *and* $\ell \geq L$ *let* $K_\ell(w) = \{i \in [\bar{n}] \mid d(u_i, w) \leq \ell\}$. *Then, it follows*
$$|K_\ell(w)| \leq \frac{1}{\beta}\left(\frac{4\ell}{L}\right)^\alpha + 1 \ .$$

2.1 The Measure of Interference I and Lower Bounds

Proof. Let p be the power assignment that allows all requests to be scheduled in a single time slot. Let furthermore (u_k, v_k) be the request with $k \in K_L(w)$ that is transmitted with minimal power p_k. As the SINR condition is satisfied for request (u_k, v_k), we get

$$\frac{1}{\beta} \frac{p_k}{d(u_k, v_k)^\alpha} \geq \sum_{\substack{i \in K_\ell(w) \\ i \neq k}} \frac{p_i}{d(u_i, v_k)^\alpha}$$

$$\geq \sum_{\substack{i \in K_\ell(w) \\ i \neq k}} \frac{p_i}{(2\ell + 2L)^\alpha}$$

$$\geq \frac{(|K_\ell(w)| - 1) \cdot p_k}{(2\ell + 2L)^\alpha}.$$

It follows

$$|K_\ell(w)| - 1 \leq \frac{1}{\beta} \left(\frac{2\ell + 2L}{d(u_k, v_k)} \right)^\alpha \leq \frac{1}{\beta} \left(\frac{4\ell}{L} \right)^\alpha.$$

$\square$

Now, let $w \in V$. We prove $I_w(C_{t,j}) = \mathcal{O}(\log n)$. W.l.o.g. let $u_1, \ldots, u_{\bar{n}}$ be ordered by increasing distance to w. Observe that for all $\ell > 0$ we have $K_\ell(w) = \{1, \ldots, x\}$ for some $x \in \mathbb{N}$ by this definition.

For $k \leq \log \bar{n} + 1$ let $S_k = [2^k] \setminus [2^{k-1}]$. Furthermore, let ℓ_k be defined as $\ell_k = \min_{i \in S_k} d(u_i, w)$. For $I_w(C_{t,j})$ follows from these definitions

$$I_w(C_{t,j}) = \sum_{i=1}^{\bar{n}} \min\left\{1, \frac{d(u_i, v_i)^\alpha}{d(u_i, w)^\alpha}\right\}$$

$$\leq \sum_{k=1}^{\log \bar{n}+1} \sum_{i \in S_k} \frac{d(u_i, v_i)^\alpha}{d(u_i, w)^\alpha} + \sum_{i \in K_L(w)} 1$$

$$\leq (2L)^\alpha \sum_{k=1}^{\log \bar{n}+1} \frac{|S_k|}{\ell_k^\alpha} + |K_L(w)|.$$

As the distances are increasing, it holds $\ell_k \geq d(u_i, w)$ for all $i \leq 2^{k-1}$. In other words $[2^{k-1}] \subseteq K_{\ell_k}(w)$.

Since we add up the interference induced by requests from $K_L(w)$ separately, we may assume $\ell_k \geq L$ for all k and apply Lemma 2.1.4 on $|K_{\ell_k}(w)|$,

2. Scheduling with the Linear Power Assignment

thus
$$2^{k-1} = |[2^{k-1}]| \leq |K_{\ell_k}(w)| \leq \left(\frac{4\ell_k}{L}\right)^\alpha + 1 \ .$$

Consequently, it follows
$$\ell_k^\alpha \geq (2^{k-1} - 1)\left(\frac{L}{4}\right)^\alpha \ .$$

Using the above results for ℓ_k^α and $|K_L(w)|$ we can bound $I_w(C_{t,j})$ by

$$(2L)^\alpha \sum_{k=1}^{\log \bar{n}+1} \frac{2^{k-1}}{(2^{k-1}-1)\left(\frac{L}{4}\right)^\alpha} + \left(\frac{4^\alpha}{\beta}+1\right) \leq 8^\alpha \sum_{k=1}^{\log \bar{n}+1} 2 + \frac{4^\alpha}{\beta} + 1 = \mathcal{O}(\log n) \ .$$

□

Earlier results (e. g., [CKM+07, GOW07]) restricted the instances often to the Euclidean plane and required α to be strictly greater than 2. Under these assumptions we can use geometric arguments to get an even better bound of $\Omega(1/\log \Delta)$ on the optimal schedule length, as we show in the following.

Theorem 2.1.5. *For a set of requests located in the Euclidean plane, if $\alpha > 2$, every schedule using an arbitrary power assignment has length at least $\Omega\left(1/\log \Delta\right)$.*

Proof. Let T denote the length of a schedule using an arbitrary power assignment. Again, we divide the requests into $\log \Delta \cdot T$ classes $C_{t,i}$. This time, we have to prove $I_w(C_{t,i}) = \mathcal{O}(1)$. Let us remark that in the Euclidean plane a ring of inner radius $L \cdot r$ and width L can be covered by $8(r+1)$ circles of radius L. If x is the center of such a circle, it follows from Lemma 2.1.4 that $|K_L(x)| \leq \frac{4^\alpha}{\beta}$. Thus we have $|K_{L(r+1)}(w) \setminus K_{Lr}(w)| \leq 8(r+1)\frac{4^\alpha}{\beta} \leq 16r\frac{4^\alpha}{\beta} = r\frac{4^{\alpha+2}}{\beta}$ for $r \geq 1$. We can bound $I_w(C_{t,j})$ by

$$I_w(C_{t,j}) \leq \sum_{r=1}^{\infty} |K_{L(r+1)}(w) \setminus K_{Lr}(w)| \cdot \frac{(2L)^\alpha}{(Lr)^\alpha} + |K_L(w)| \ .$$

Using the above result we get

$$I_w(C_{t,j}) \leq 2^\alpha \frac{4^{\alpha+2}}{\beta} \sum_{r=1}^{\infty} r^{1-\alpha} + \frac{4^\alpha}{\beta} \leq \frac{4^\alpha}{\beta}\left(2^\alpha 4^2 \frac{\alpha-1}{\alpha-2} + 1\right) = \mathcal{O}(1) \ .$$

2.2 Upper Bounds for the Linear Power Assignment

The measure of interference introduced in the last section enables us to design randomized algorithms using the linear power assignment. Before we turn towards the algorithms we simplify the SINR constraint to avoid notational clutter.

For a request pair (u_i, v_i) the linear power assignment sets the power $p_i = c \cdot (u_i, v_i)^\alpha$ for some fixed $c \geq \beta N$. If $\mathcal{R}$ is a set of requests that can be scheduled in one time slot, we have for all nodes v' with $(u', v') \in \mathcal{R}$

$$\sum_{\substack{(u,v) \in \mathcal{R} \\ (u,v) \neq (u',v')}} \frac{c \cdot d(u,v)^\alpha}{d(u,v')^\alpha} \leq \frac{c}{\beta} - N \ .$$

Since $\beta > 1$ we can write equivalently

$$I_{v'}(\mathcal{R}) = \sum_{(u,v) \in \mathcal{R}} \min\left\{1, \frac{d(u,v)^\alpha}{d(u,v')^\alpha}\right\} \leq \frac{1}{\beta} - \frac{N}{c} \ . \tag{2.3}$$

For simplicity of notation we replace $\frac{1}{\beta} - \frac{N}{c}$ by $\frac{1}{\beta'}$ in the following proofs.

The idea of our basic algorithm (Algorithm 1) is that each sender decides randomly in each time slot if it tries to transmit until it is successful. The probability of transmission is set to $\frac{1}{2\beta' I}$ and is not changed throughout the process.

Algorithm 1 A simple single-hop algorithm

1: **while** packet has not been successfully transmitted **do**
2:   try transmitting with probability $\frac{1}{2\beta' I}$
3: **end while**

Theorem 2.2.1. *Algorithm 1 yields a schedule of length at most $\mathcal{O}(I \log n)$ whp.*

Proof. We first consider the probability of success for a fixed request (u_k, v_k) in a single step of the algorithm. Let X_i, $i \in [n]$, be the 0/1 random variable

2. Scheduling with the Linear Power Assignment

indicating if sender u_i tries to transmit in this step. Assume a sender u_k tries to transmit in this step, i.e., $X_k = 1$. To make this attempt successful, the interference constraint (Equation 2.3) has to be satisfied. We can express this event as $Z \leq 1/\beta'$ where Z is defined by

$$Z = \sum_{\substack{i \in [n] \\ i \neq k}} \min\left\{1, \frac{d(u_i, v_i)^\alpha}{d(u_i, v_k)^\alpha}\right\} X_i \ .$$

We have $\mathbf{E}[Z] \leq 1/2\beta'$ and thus we can use Markov's inequality to bound the probability that this packet cannot be transmitted successfully by

$$\mathbf{Pr}\left[Z \geq \frac{1}{\beta'}\right] \leq \mathbf{Pr}\left[Z \geq 2\mathbf{E}[Z]\right] \leq \frac{1}{2} \ .$$

To make the transmission successful the two events $X_k = 1$ and $Z \leq 1/\beta'$ have to occur. Since they are independent it holds that

$$\begin{aligned}\mathbf{Pr}\left[X_k = 1, Z \leq \frac{1}{\beta'}\right] &= \mathbf{Pr}\left[X_k = 1\right] \cdot \mathbf{Pr}\left[Z \leq \frac{1}{\beta'}\right] \\ &\geq \frac{1}{2\beta' I}\left(1 - \frac{1}{2}\right) \\ &= \frac{1}{4\beta' I} \ .\end{aligned}$$

Thus, the probability for packet k not to be successfully transmitted in $(k_0 + 1)4\beta' I \ln n$ independent repeats of such a step is therefore at most

$$\left(1 - \frac{1}{4\beta' I}\right)^{(k_0+1)4\beta' I \ln n} \leq e^{-(k_0+1)\ln n} = n^{-(k_0+1)} \ .$$

Applying a union bound we get an overall bound on the probability that one of n packets is not successfully transmitted in these independent repeats by n^{-k_0}. This means all senders are successful within $\mathcal{O}(I \log n)$ steps whp. □

An obvious disadvantage of the basic algorithm is that the probability of transmission stays the same throughout the process. We can improve this bound by increasing the probability of transmission after some transmissions have successfully taken place. We need the following weighted Chernoff bound that can deal with dependent random variables.

2.2 Upper Bounds for the Linear Power Assignment

Lemma 2.2.2. *Let $X_1, \ldots, X_n$ be 0/1 random variables for which there exists $p \in [0,1]$ such that for all $k \in [n]$ and all $a_1, \ldots, a_{k-1} \in \{0,1\}$*

$$\Pr[X_k = 1 \mid X_1 = a_1, \ldots X_{k-1} = a_{k-1}] \leq p \ . \tag{2.4}$$

Let furthermore $w_1, \ldots, w_n$ be reals in $(0,1]$ and $\mu \geq p \sum w_i$. Then the weighted Chernoff bound

$$\Pr\left[\sum_{i=1}^n w_i X_i \geq (1+\delta)\mu\right] \leq \left(\frac{e^\delta}{(1+\delta)^{(1+\delta)}}\right)^\mu$$

holds.

Proof. To show this bound, a standard proof for the weighted Chernoff bound [Rag88] can be adapted. By using the definition of expectation and repeatedly applying Equation 2.4, one can show that

$$\mathbf{E}\left[e^{tX}\right] \leq \prod_{i=1}^n \left(pe^{tw_i} + 1 - p\right) \ ,$$

although random variables are no more independent. In the original proof no other step makes use of the independence. □

This bound can be used to analyze the more sophisticated Algorithm 2. This algorithm assigns random delays to all packets. The maximum delay is decreased depending on I^{curr}, which denotes the measure of interference that is induced by the requests that have not been scheduled at this point.

Algorithm 2 An $\mathcal{O}(I + \log^2 n)$ whp algorithm

1: **while** $I^{\mathrm{curr}} \geq \log n$ **do**
2:    $J := I^{\mathrm{curr}}$
3:    **while** $I^{\mathrm{curr}} \geq \frac{J}{2}$ **do**
4:       **if** packet i has not been successfully transmitted **then**
5:          assign a delay $1 \leq \delta_i \leq 16e\beta' J$ i. u. r.
6:          try transmission after waiting the delay
7:       **end if**
8:    **end while**
9: **end while**
10: execute algorithm Algorithm 1

2. Scheduling with the Linear Power Assignment

The algorithm works as follows: The measure of interference is reduced to a half of its initial value during one iteration of the outer *while* loop by repeatedly assigning random delays to the packets. This is repeated until we have $I^{\text{curr}} < \log n$ and the basic algorithm is applied.

Our first observation is that reducing I^{curr} by factor 2 takes $\mathcal{O}(I^{\text{curr}})$ scheduling steps whp.

Lemma 2.2.3. *During one iteration of the outer* while *loop of Algorithm 2, the inner* while *loop is executed at most $k_0 + 2$ times with probability at least $1 - n^{-k_0}$ for all constants k_0.*

Proof. Let us first consider a single iteration of this loop. We assume all senders are taking part as if none has been successful during this iteration of the outer *while* loop yet. We only benefit from any previous success.

Observe, if the senders of a set S are transmitting and there is a collision for packet i, it holds

$$\sum_{\substack{j \in S \\ j < i}} \min\left\{1, \frac{d(u_j, v_j)^\alpha}{d(u_j, v_i)^\alpha}\right\} > \frac{1}{2\beta'} \quad \text{or} \quad \sum_{\substack{j \in S \\ j > i}} \min\left\{1, \frac{d(u_j, v_j)^\alpha}{d(u_j, v_i)^\alpha}\right\} > \frac{1}{2\beta'} .$$

In the first case let $Y_i^< = 1$, in the second one $Y_i^> = 1$. We now show that the random variables $Y_1^<, \ldots, Y_n^<$ fulfill Equation 2.4 for $p = \frac{1}{8e}$. Let us fix $k \in [n]$ and $a_1, \ldots, a_{k-1} \in \{0, 1\}$. We have to show

$$\mathbf{Pr}\left[Y_k^< = 1 \mid Y_1^< = a_1, \ldots, Y_{k-1}^< = a_{k-1}\right] \leq p .$$

Since the delays δ_i are drawn independently they can be considered as if they were drawn one after the other in order $\delta_1, \delta_2, \ldots$. Then the value of $Y_i^<$ would already be determined after drawing δ_i by definition. In other words: The values of $\delta_1, \ldots, \delta_{k-1}$ already determine the values of $Y_1^<, \ldots, Y_{k-1}^<$. It follows that there is a subset $M \subseteq [16e\beta'J]^{k-1}$ of delay values such that $Y_1^< = a_1, \ldots, Y_{k-1}^< = a_{k-1}$ iff $(\delta_1, \ldots, \delta_{k-1}) \in M$.

Now let X_i be a 0/1 random variable for $i \in [k-1]$ such that $X_i = 1$ iff $\delta_i = \delta_k$. We can observe that for all $(b_1, \ldots, b_{k-1}) \in [16e\beta'J]^{k-1}$ it holds

$$\mathbf{E}\left[X_i \mid \delta_1 = b_1, \ldots, \delta_{k-1} = b_{k-1}\right] = \frac{1}{16e\beta'J} .$$

2.2 Upper Bounds for the Linear Power Assignment

Define furthermore

$$Z_k^< = \sum_{i=1}^{k-1} \min\left\{1, \frac{d(u_i, v_i)^\alpha}{d(u_i, v_k)^\alpha}\right\} X_i$$

with $\mathbf{E}\left[Z_k^< \mid \delta_1 = b_1, \ldots, \delta_{k-1} = b_{k-1}\right] \leq \frac{1}{16e\beta'}$. Now it follows that

$$\begin{aligned}
\mathbf{Pr}\left[Y_k^< = 1 \mid \delta_1 = b_1, \ldots, \delta_{j-1} = b_{k-1}\right] \\
= \mathbf{Pr}\left[Z_k^< > \frac{1}{2\beta'} \,\middle|\, \delta_1 = b_1, \ldots, \delta_{k-1} = b_{k-1}\right] \\
\leq 2\beta' \mathbf{E}\left[Z_k^< \mid \delta_1 = b_1, \ldots, \delta_{k-1} = b_{k-1}\right] \\
= \frac{1}{8e} = p \ .
\end{aligned}$$

Applying the law of alternatives yields

$$\begin{aligned}
&\mathbf{Pr}\left[Y_k^< = 1 \mid Y_1^< = a_1, \ldots, Y_{k-1}^< = a_{k-1}\right] \\
&= \sum_{(b_1,\ldots,b_{k-1})\in M} \mathbf{Pr}\left[\delta_1 = b_1, \ldots, \delta_{k-1} = b_{k-1} \mid Y_1^< = a_1, \ldots, Y_{k-1}^< = a_{k-1}\right] \\
&\quad \cdot \mathbf{Pr}\left[Y_k^< = 1 \mid \delta_1 = b_1, \ldots, \delta_{k-1} = b_{k-1}\right] \\
&\leq p \ .
\end{aligned}$$

Thus, for $w \in V$, we may apply Lemma 2.2.2 on $I_w^<$ defined as

$$I_w^< = \sum_{i=1}^{n} \min\left\{1, \frac{d(u_i, v_i)^\alpha}{d(u_i, w)^\alpha}\right\} Y_i^< \ .$$

This random variable indicates the remaining measure of interference that is caused by these collisions. Setting $\delta = 2e - 1$ and $\mu = \frac{J}{8e}$ Lemma 2.2.2 states

$$\mathbf{Pr}\left[I_w^< \geq \frac{J}{4}\right] \leq 2^{-\frac{J}{4}} \leq n^{-1} \ .$$

Now consider the situation after $k_0 + 2$ iterations of the inner *while* loop. Since these are independent repeats we have

$$\mathbf{Pr}\left[I_w^< \geq \frac{J}{4}\right] \leq n^{-(k_0+2)} \ .$$

2. Scheduling with the Linear Power Assignment

With a symmetric argument this also applies to $I_j^>$. For a sender that has not been successful we have $Z_j^< + Z_j^> \geq 1$. This means we have the bound $I_w^{\text{curr}} \leq I_w^< + I_w^>$. For the remaining measure of interference $I^{\text{curr}} = \max_{w \in V} I_w^{\text{curr}}$ we can conclude

$$\begin{aligned}
\Pr\left[I^{\text{curr}} \geq \frac{J}{2}\right] &\leq \sum_{w \in V} \Pr\left[I_w^{\text{curr}} \geq \frac{J}{2}\right] \\
&\leq \sum_{w \in V} \Pr\left[I_w^< \geq \frac{J}{4} \text{ or } I_w^< \geq \frac{J}{4}\right] \\
&\leq n\left(n^{-(k_0+2)} + n^{-(k_0+2)}\right) \\
&\leq n^{-k_0} .
\end{aligned}$$

$\square$

Using the previous lemma, we can bound the numbers of steps that are generated in the *while* loops.

Theorem 2.2.4. *Algorithm 2 generates a schedule of length at most $\mathcal{O}(I + \log^2 n)$ steps whp.*

Proof. Let T_k denote the number of scheduling steps generated in the k-th execution of the outer *while* loop. From the previous lemma we know that

$$\Pr\left[v_k \geq (k_0+3)\,16e\beta'\frac{1}{2^{k-1}}I\right] \leq \frac{1}{n^{k_0+1}} .$$

Let furthermore U denote the number of scheduling steps generated in the execution of Algorithm 1. As shown in Lemma 2.2.1, it holds that

$$\Pr\left[U \geq (k_0+2)\,4\beta'\ln n \log n\right] \leq \frac{1}{n^{k_0+1}} .$$

Thus the total number of steps generated in the *while* loops $\sum_k v_k + U$ can be estimated by

$$\Pr\left[\sum_k v_k + U \geq (k_0+3)\,32e\beta'I + (k_0+2)\,4\beta'\ln n \log n\right]$$

$$\leq \Pr\left[\bigvee_k v_k \geq (k_0+3)\,16e\beta'\frac{1}{2^{k-1}}I \vee U \geq (k_0+2)\,4\beta'\ln n \log n\right]$$

$$\leq \sum_k \mathbf{Pr}\left[v_k \geq (k_0+3)\,16e\beta'\frac{1}{2^{k-1}}I\right] + \mathbf{Pr}\left[U \geq (k_0+2)\,4\beta'\ln n \log n\right]$$

$$\leq \sum_k \frac{1}{n^{k_0+1}} + \frac{1}{n^{k_0+1}}$$

$$\leq (\log n + 1)\frac{1}{n^{k_0+1}}$$

$$\leq \frac{1}{n^{k_0}}\,.$$

This means the total number of steps is upper bounded by

$$(k_0+3)\,32e\beta'I + (k_0+2)\,4\beta'\ln n \log n = O(I + \log^2 n)$$

with probability at least $1 - \frac{1}{n^{k_0}}$. □

In sufficiently dense instances, i.e., $I \geq \log^2 n$, this algorithm with high probability yields a constant-factor approximation to the optimal schedule length restricted to the linear power assignment. Compared to the length with an optimal power assignment the approximation factor then is $\mathcal{O}(\log \Delta \cdot \log n)$ whp for general metrics resp. $\mathcal{O}(\log \Delta)$ for the two-dimensional Euclidean plane.

Algorithm 1 can be implemented in a distributed way losing a factor $\mathcal{O}(\log n)$ in the following way. In contrast to the centralized problem, the nodes do not know the correct value of I, thus, they do not know their transmission probability. Now in the distributed setting the algorithm executes in each *while* iteration $\log n$ steps, where in each of these steps the transmission probability is halved, that is, starting by $1/2\beta'$ down to $1/2\beta' n$. Algorithm 2 can be modified analogously, leading to a schedule of length $\mathcal{O}(\log n \cdot (I + \log^2 n))$ whp.

A more detailed discussion about distributed approaches can be found in [KV10].

2.3 Extensions for Multi-hop Scheduling and Routing

The multi-hop variant of the interference scheduling problem was first stated by Chafekar et al. [CKM+07] as *Cross-Layer Latency Minimization* (CLM)

2. Scheduling with the Linear Power Assignment

problem. Given n source destination pairs (u_i, v_i), the objective is to find paths from u_i to v_i to send the packets along, powers for each transmission, and a schedule assigning the hops to time slots minimizing the time until the last packet is delivered. In this section we will present how the measure of interference introduced in Section 2.1 and the single-hop algorithms from Section 2.2 can be extended to multi-hop scheduling.

2.3.1 Multi-hop Scheduling with Fixed Paths

At first we consider the paths to be fixed. In this case the task is to schedule a set of requests $\mathcal{R}$ consisting of n pairs of nodes that lie on paths, respecting dependencies such that one request may not be served before the ones lying earlier on the path have been served. Obviously, the bounds on the measure of interference proven in Section 2.1 still hold. However, we additionally express these dependencies in the dilation D, which is the maximum path length. Of course, any schedule using an arbitrary power assignment has length at least D.

In a naive approach to solve this problem we could treat the multi-hop problem as a concatenation of D single-hop problems and schedule each of them separately. This schedule has a length of $\mathcal{O}((I + \log^2 n)D)$ steps whp. Algorithm 3 extends this idea by assigning a random delay to each packet. This technique has also been applied for scheduling in wired networks, e.g., by Leighton et al. [LMR94].

By this shift, a number of time frames is created and to each of them a set of requests $\mathcal{R}_i$ is assigned. Due to the random delay the measure of interference $I(\mathcal{R}_i)$ is sufficiently balanced between those time frames. As different hops that lie on the same path are assigned to different time frames, our single-hop algorithm can be used to generate a schedule for each time frame.

Algorithm 3 Fixed path multi-hop scheduling

1: **for all** $i \in [n]$ **do**
2:     assign a delay $1 \leq \delta_i \leq \frac{2eI}{\log^2 n}$ i. u. r.
3: **end for**
4: **for all** $1 \leq t \leq \frac{2eI}{\log^2 n} + D$ **do**
5:     execute Algorithm 2 on all hops (i, j) with $\delta_i + j = t$
6: **end for**

2.3 Extensions for Multi-hop Scheduling and Routing

Theorem 2.3.1. *The schedule generated by Algorithm 3 has length* $\mathcal{O}(I + D \log^2 n)$ *whp.*

Proof. Let $I_w(\mathcal{R}_t)$ denote the random variable of I caused by all requests assigned to time frame t. Further, let $P_{i,j}$ denote the i-th node on the j-th path and let $X_{i,j,t}$ be a 0/1 random variable such that $X_{i,j,t} = 1$ iff $\delta_i + j = t$. Then it holds

$$I_w(\mathcal{R}_t) = \sum_{i,j} \min\left\{1, \frac{d(P_{i,j-1}, P_{i,j})^\alpha}{d(P_{i,j-1}, w)^\alpha}\right\} X_{i,j,t} \ .$$

As we have $\Pr[X_{i,j,t} = 1] = \log^2 n / 2eI$, we can bound the expectation of $I_w(\mathcal{R}_t)$ by $\mathbf{E}[I_w(\mathcal{R}_t)] \leq \log^2 n / 2e$. For fixed t the random variables $X_{i,j,t}$ are *negatively associated* as defined by Dubhashi and Ranjan [DR98]. So a Chernoff bound is applicable. For all $k_2 \geq 1$ it holds that

$$\Pr\left[I_w(\mathcal{R}_i) \geq k_2 \log^2 n\right] \leq 2^{-k_2 \log^2 n} \leq 2^{-k_2 \log n} = n^{-k_2} \ .$$

Let T_t denote the schedule length that is used by Algorithm 2 to schedule $\mathcal{R}_t$. We proved in Theorem 2.2.4 that for all constants k_1 and k_2 there is a constant k_0 such that

$$\Pr\left[T_t \geq k_0 k_2 \log^2 n \ \Big|\ \max_{w \in V} I_w(\mathcal{R}_t) \leq k_2 \log^2 n\right] \leq \frac{1}{n^{k_1}} \ .$$

Applying a union bound we get the probability that none of the $2eI/\log^2 n + D \leq n$ random variables T_t exceeds $k_0 k_2 \log^2 n$. In total, Algorithm 3 generates a schedule length of $\mathcal{O}(I + D \log^2 n)$ whp. □

2.3.2 Finding Optimal Paths (Routing)

To find optimal paths an approach first used by Srinivasan and Teo [ST97] for wired networks can be adapted, solving an *Integer Linear Program* (ILP) approximately by using relaxation and randomized rounding. Chafekar et al. [CKM+07] also use this technique as a part of their CLM algorithm.

First, let us formalize the problem of finding paths such that $\max\{I, D\}$ is minimal as ILP. We introduce a set of edges $E \subseteq V \times V$ which describes the set of links that may be used. Let furthermore $N_{\text{in}}(v)$ resp. $N_{\text{out}}(v)$ denote the incoming resp. outgoing edges from v.

2. Scheduling with the Linear Power Assignment

Minimize w subject to:

$$\forall i \in [n] \qquad \sum_{e \in N_{\text{out}}(s_i)} y(i,e) - \sum_{e \in N_{\text{in}}(s_i)} y(i,e) = 1 \qquad (2.5\text{a})$$

$$\forall i \in [n], v \in V \setminus \{u_i, v_i\} \quad \sum_{e \in N_{\text{out}}(v)} y(i,e) - \sum_{e \in N_{\text{in}}(v)} y(i,e) = 0 \qquad (2.5\text{b})$$

$$\forall i \in [n] \qquad \sum_{e \in E} y(i,e) \le w \qquad (2.5\text{c})$$

$$\forall v \in V \qquad \sum_{i \in [n]} \sum_{e' = (u', v')} y(i, e') \min \left\{ 1, \frac{d(u', v')^\alpha}{d(u', v)^\alpha} \right\} \le w$$
$$(2.5\text{d})$$

$$\forall i \in [n], e \in E \qquad y(i,e) \in \{0,1\} \qquad (2.5\text{e})$$

This ILP is designed to minimize $w = \max\{I, D\}$ as follows. Condition 2.5d ensures that $I \le w$ whereas Condition 2.5c ensures $D \le w$. By leaving out Condition 2.5e, this ILP can be relaxed to an LP which then describes a multi-commodity flow problem.

This LP can be solved in polynomial time. Afterwards we can use the LP result to approximate a solution of the ILP, by selecting paths of length at most $2w$ and applying the technique of randomized rounding [RT87]. In a simple analysis we find out the following. If I^* and D^* denote the values such that $\max\{I, D\}$ is minimal – which is the optimal solution for the ILP – we calculate paths such that $I = \mathcal{O}(I^* \log n)$ whp and $D \le 2D^*$ this way.

2.3.3 Consequences for the CLM Problem

Let us combine our results to get an approximation algorithm for the CLM problem as stated by Chafekar et al. [CKM+07]. Assume there is an optimal choice of paths, powers and a schedule such that the latency is T. Let the measure of interference caused by these paths be denoted by $I^\dagger$ and their dilation by $D^\dagger$. In Section 2.1 we showed that $I^\dagger = \mathcal{O}(\log \Delta \cdot \log n \cdot T)$. Obviously $D^\dagger = \mathcal{O}(T)$ holds, too.

If I^* and D^* are the values such that $\max\{I, D\}$ is minimal, our path selection algorithm chooses paths such that $I = \mathcal{O}(I^* \log n)$ whp and $D = \mathcal{O}(D^*)$. A schedule by Algorithm 3 using these paths has length $\mathcal{O}(I + D \log^2 n) = \mathcal{O}(I^* \log n + D^* \log^2 n) = \mathcal{O}((I^\dagger + D^\dagger) \log^2 n) = \mathcal{O}(\log \Delta \cdot \log^3 n \cdot T)$

2.3 Extensions for Multi-hop Scheduling and Routing

whp. Thus we reached an approximation factor of $\mathcal{O}(\log \Delta \cdot \log^3 n)$ whp. For instances restricted to the Euclidean plane, we even get an approximation factor for $\mathcal{O}(\log \Delta \cdot \log^2 n)$ whp.

2. Scheduling with the Linear Power Assignment

Chapter 3

Oblivious Power Assignments and the Bidirectional Model

In this chapter we analyze the interference scheduling problem for oblivious power assignments, i.e., $p_i = \phi(d(u_i, v_i))$ with $\phi : [1, \Delta] \to (0, \infty)$. In Section 3.1 we show that in the unidirectional problem each oblivious power assignment can perform poorly compared to the optimal schedule. We further present a single instance in which each schedule using an oblivious power assignment is at least a factor $\Omega(\sqrt{\log \log \Delta})$ longer than an optimal schedule.

When studying the bidirectional model, the most common power assignments (namely the uniform and the linear assignment) still yield poor worst case schedules. This does not hold for any oblivious power assignment. Section 3.2 is an in-depth analysis that a schedule using the square root assignment is at most a polylogartihmic factor longer than the optimal one. We present how to decompose general metrics first to tree metrics (Section 3.2.3) and then into star metrics (Section 3.2.4). In Section 3.2.6 we analyze scheduling on those star metrics. We finally present an efficient approximation algorithm in Section 3.3.

3.1 The Gap of Oblivious Power Schemes

In the unidirectional case any oblivious power assignment can perform poorly when compared to an optimal power scheme. To prove this we construct a family of instances for a given function f such that using f requires at least $\Omega(n)$ colors or schedule steps while an optimal power assignment needs only

3. Oblivious Power Assignments and the Bidirectional Model

$\mathcal{O}(1)$ steps.

Theorem 3.1.1. *For any oblivious power assignment p there exists a family of instances with n directed communication requests needing $\Omega(n)$ steps when using p, but only a constant number of steps when using an optimal power assignment.*

Proof. Let $d_i = d(u_i, v_i)$ and let p_i be any oblivious power assignment defined by $\phi : \mathbb{R}_{>0} \to \mathbb{R}_{>0}$, that is, $p_i = \phi(d_i)$. We distinguish three cases. In the first case, we assume that ϕ is asymptotically unbounded, that is, for every $c > 0$ and every $d_0 > 0$ there exists a value $d > d_0$ with $\phi(d) > c$.

We consider the following family of instances as illustrated in Figure 3.1. They consist of n pairs (u_i, v_i), with distances d_i between two nodes of a pair and $M \cdot y_i$ between neighboring pairs. Depending on β, we choose M as a suitable constant that is large enough to get along with different values of β.

Formally, this kind of instance can be defined by $u_1, v_1, \ldots, u_n, v_n \in \mathbb{R}$ such that

$$u_i = \begin{cases} 0 & \text{if } i = 1 \\ v_{i-1} + M \cdot y_i & \text{otherwise} \end{cases} \quad \text{and} \quad v_i = u_i + d_i \ .$$

We now define the distances d_i and y_i between the nodes recursively depending on the function ϕ:

$$y_i = 2(d_{i-1} + y_{i-1}).$$

Given $d_1, \ldots, d_{i-1}$ and y_i, we choose d_i such that $d_i \geq y_i$ and

$$\phi(d_i) \geq y_i^\alpha \frac{\phi(d_j)}{d_j^\alpha} \quad \text{for all } j < i.$$

This is always possible since ϕ is asymptotically unbounded. By this construction it is ensured that a pair k is exposed to high interference by pairs

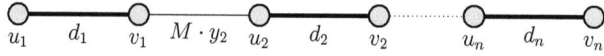

Figure 3.1: A visualization of the instances of asymptotically unbounded ϕ. d_i and y_i are chosen depending on ϕ.

3.1 The Gap of Oblivious Power Schemes

with larger indices. To show this, let $S \subseteq [n]$ be a set of indices of pairs that can be scheduled together in one step and let $k = \min S$. For $i \in S \setminus \{k\}$ holds

$$d(u_i, v_k) = \sum_{j=k+1}^{i-1} d_j + \sum_{j=k+1}^{i} M \cdot y_j \leq 2M \cdot \sum_{j=k}^{i} y_j \leq 2M \cdot \sum_{j=k}^{i} \frac{1}{2^{i-j}} y_i \leq 4M \cdot y_i \ .$$

Since all pairs in S can be scheduled in one step the SINR condition is satisfied for pair k and it holds

$$\beta \sum_{i \in S \setminus \{k\}} \frac{p_i}{d(u_i, v_k)^\alpha} \leq \frac{p_k}{d(u_k, v_k)^\alpha} = \frac{\phi(d_k)}{d_k^\alpha} \ .$$

Putting these facts together yields

$$\frac{1}{\beta} \cdot \frac{\phi(d_k)}{d_k^\alpha} \geq \sum_{i \in S \setminus \{k\}} \frac{p_i}{d(u_i, v_k)^\alpha} \geq \sum_{i \in S \setminus \{k\}} \frac{y_i^\alpha \frac{\phi(d_k)}{d_k^\alpha}}{(4M \cdot y_i)^\alpha} = \frac{|S|-1}{(4M)^\alpha} \frac{\phi(d_k)}{d_k^\alpha} \ .$$

This implies $|S| \leq \frac{(4M)^\alpha}{\beta} + 1$, which means there are at least $\frac{\beta}{(4M)^\alpha + \beta} n = \Omega(n)$ schedule steps needed when using $p_i = \phi(d_i^\alpha)$.

On the other hand for these instances there is a power assignment, $p_i = \sqrt{2^i}$, such that there is a schedule of constant length. This is caused by the fact that for all instances described it holds that $y_i \leq d_i$ and $y_{i+1} \geq 2d_i$. Thus, for any link k the interference by the ones with higher index as well as the ones with lower index form a geometric series. This means a constant fraction of all links may be assigned in the same schedule slot and therefore there exists a schedule of constant length.

In the second case, we assume that ϕ is asymptotically bounded from above by some value $c > 0$ but does not converge to 0. In this case, there exists a value $b \in (0, c]$ such that for every $d_0 > 0$ there exists a value $d > d_0$ with $\phi(d) \in [b, 2b]$. Let $M > 1$ be a suitable constant. We choose n numbers $d_1, \ldots, d_n$ satisfying the properties a) $\phi(d_i) \in [b, 2b]$, for $1 \leq i \leq n$, and b) $d_i \geq M \cdot d_{i-1}$, for $2 \leq i \leq n$. We set $u_i = -d_i/2$ and $v_i = d_i/2$. This yields a sequence of nested pairs on the line (see Figure 3.2). The power assignment defined by ϕ essentially corresponds to the uniform power assignment so that only a constant number of requests can be scheduled simultaneously. To show this, let $S \subseteq [n]$ be a set of indices of pairs that can be scheduled in one step

3. Oblivious Power Assignments and the Bidirectional Model

and let $k = \max S$. For $i \in S \setminus \{k\}$ holds

$$d(u_i, v_k) = \frac{d_i}{2} + \frac{d_k}{2} < d_k \ .$$

The SINR condition for k yields

$$\beta \sum_{i \in S \setminus \{k\}} \frac{p_i}{d(u_i, v_k)^\alpha} \leq \frac{p_k}{d(u_k, v_k)^\alpha} = \frac{\phi(d_k)}{d_k^\alpha} \leq \frac{2b}{d_k^\alpha} \ .$$

Combining the last equations gives

$$\frac{1}{\beta} \cdot \frac{2b}{d_k^\alpha} \geq \sum_{i \in S \setminus \{k\}} \frac{p_i}{d(u_i, v_k)^\alpha} \geq \sum_{i \in S \setminus \{k\}} \frac{b}{d_k^\alpha} = (|S| - 1) \frac{b}{d_k^\alpha}$$

and so $|S| \leq \frac{2}{\beta} + 1$. This implies ϕ yields a schedule of length at least $\frac{\beta}{2+\beta} n = \Omega(n)$ for this request set. In contrast, if M is chosen sufficiently large then the square root power assignment can schedule all these requests simultaneously.

Finally, in the third case, $\lim \phi(d) = 0$, we again construct a sequence of nested pairs analogously to second case but replacing condition a) by the condition $\phi(d_i) \leq \phi(d_{i-1})$. Analogously to the second case, the power assignment defined by ϕ allows only for scheduling a constant number of pairs simultaneously while the square root assignment can schedule all pairs simultaneously. □

This result shows that the dependence on Δ is necessary for nontrivial results. The following theorem shows that there is a gap of at least

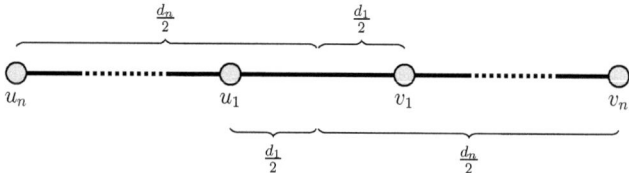

Figure 3.2: A visualization of the instances where ϕ is asymptotically bounded from above by some positive constant. Again, d_i and y_i are chosen depending on ϕ.

3.1 The Gap of Oblivious Power Schemes

$\Omega(\sqrt{\log \log \Delta})$ between oblivious and optimal power assignments.

Theorem 3.1.2. *An instance of the interference scheduling problem exists such that every schedule using an oblivious power function needs at least $\Omega(\sqrt{\log \log \Delta})$ more steps than the optimal schedule.*

Proof. In this proof we construct an instance that can be scheduled in a constant number of rounds by a non-oblivious power assignment, but every oblivious power assignment needs at least $\Omega(\sqrt{\log \log \Delta})$ steps. The instance consist of two nearly identical requests sets, only the role of sender and receiver in each request is exchanged. More formally, let $x_1 = 1$, $y_i = x_i^2$ and $x_{i+1} = 2y_i$ for every $i \in [n]$. Let the request set R_1 consist of the requests (u_i, v_i) described by

$$u_i = \begin{cases} 0 & \text{if } i = 1 \\ -\sum_{j=2}^{i} x_j & \text{otherwise} \end{cases} \quad \text{and} \quad v_i = \sum_{j=1}^{i} y_i$$

and let R_2 consist of requests (u'_i, v'_i) with

$$u'_i = M + \sum_{j=1}^{i} y_i \quad \text{and} \quad v'_i = \begin{cases} M & \text{if } i = 1 \\ M - \sum_{j=2}^{i} x_j & \text{otherwise} \end{cases},$$

where M denotes a constant large enough that interferences between requests from R_1 and R_2 become negligible. Since for all $i \in [n]$ holds $d(u_i, v_i) = d(u'_i, v'_i)$, every oblivious power assignment uses the same power p_i for request (u_i, v_i) and (u'_i, v'_i).

Let T denote the schedule under an arbitrary, fixed oblivious power assignment. In this schedule there must be a step where at least n/T requests from R_1 are scheduled. Let $\hat{R} \subseteq [n]$ denote their indices. Let $i, j \in \hat{R}$ with $i < j$. The SINR-constraint states

$$\beta \frac{p_i}{d(u_i, v_j)^\alpha} \leq \frac{p_j}{d(u_j, v_j)^\alpha} .$$

Using $d(u_i, v_j) \leq x_j$ and $d(u_j, v_j) \geq y_j = x_j^2$ we get

$$\beta \frac{p_i}{x_j^\alpha} \leq \frac{p_j}{x_j^{2\alpha}} ,$$

which implies $p_i \leq p_j/\beta x_j^\alpha$. With $d(u'_j, v'_i) \leq 2x_j$, the interference from (u'_j, v'_j)

41

3. Oblivious Power Assignments and the Bidirectional Model

on (u'_i, v'_i) is

$$\beta \frac{p_j}{d(u'_j, v'_i)^\alpha} \geq \beta \frac{p_j}{(2x_j)^\alpha} \geq \frac{\beta^2 p_i}{2^\alpha} > \frac{p_i}{d(u'_i, v'_i)^\alpha}.$$

Thus, for every $i \neq j$, $i, j \in \hat{R}$, the requests (u'_i, v'_i) and (u'_j, v'_j) cannot be scheduled in the same step. In fact, for every $i \in \hat{R}$, (u'_i, v'_i) must be assigned to a different schedule step. This yields $T \geq \left|\hat{R}\right|$ and it follows $T \geq \sqrt{n} = \sqrt{\Omega(\log \log \Delta)}$. □

3.2 The Square Root Assignment

In this section we extend the interference scheduling problem for bidirectional communication. A straight forward adaption from the proof of Theorem 3.1.1 from the previous chapter shows that bounded, linear and superlinear power assignments still produce schedules that are a factor $\Omega(n)$ away from optimal schedules. However, for sublinear functions such an adaption is not possible. In fact, we will show in this chapter that there exists a sublinear function, namely the square root function, which allows to minimize the number of colors up to a polylogarithmic factor for bidirectional communication. For the square root power assignment, which we will denote in the following with $\bar{p}$, we prove the following theorem.

Theorem 3.2.1. *For any set of n bidirectional requests, the square root power assignment admits a schedule that is at most $\mathcal{O}(\log^{3.5+\alpha} n)$ times longer than an optimal schedule.*

In this chapter we will ensure that the SINR constraint is fulfilled with strict inequality. As a consequence we will ignore the noise N, i.e., we set $N = 0$, as we can scale all powers up to overcome any noise eventually. Clearly, such a scaling might be wasteful or infeasible in practice, but this aspect is beyond our analysis.

The first major observation for the proofs that is used throughout the remainder of the chapter is that we can "play" with the SINR threshold β in the sense that changing the SINR threshold by a constant factor can only change the the length of a feasible schedule by a logarithmic factor. Suppose that one is given a schedule or coloring for small value β' but the actual

3.2 The Square Root Assignment

threshold parameter of the model is β. Then we can sample pairs from a color class with probability $\mathcal{O}(\beta/\beta')$. In such a sample many of the sampled pairs (say a constant fraction) will have a sufficiently small interference so that they can be scheduled. Hence, from a color class with k pairs one round of sampling schedules $\mathcal{O}(k \cdot \beta/\beta')$ pairs. Repeating this process for $\mathcal{O}(\beta'/\beta \log n)$ rounds schedules all pairs from a class with high probability. Because of this technique, which we will present in Section 3.2.1, the proofs in the following sections assume that we are given an instance of the problem that can be scheduled in one round with sufficiently high threshold β. Then we show that the square root assignment schedules a large fraction of this instance with threshold β' that may be a polylogarithmic factor smaller than β.

The second approach which we use to simplify the problem will be presented in Section 3.2.2. We reduce the scheduling from pairs of nodes to scheduling single nodes by splitting up the communication pairs. In this *node-loss scheduling problem* a so called loss parameter is used to keep track of the signal fading between the communication partners.

This is followed by the main part of the proof of Theorem 3.2.1, which consists of two major parts. In Sections 3.2.3 and 3.2.4 we present how to decompose general metrics first to tree metrics and from there finally to star metrics. In Section 3.2.6 we then analyze the node-loss scheduling in detail on stars, finishing the proof of the theorem.

3.2.1 Scaling the SINR Threshold

Consider an instance of the interference scheduling problem in the directed or bidirectional variant with n requests. Suppose both the coloring c and the power assignment p are fixed such that the SINR constraints are satisfied with threshold β. We show the existence of a coloring c' that for the same power assignment p satisfies the SINR constraints with a more restrictive threshold $\beta' > \beta$ and uses only $\mathcal{O}(\beta'/\beta \log n)$ times the number of colors in c. Our analysis focuses on the bidirectional variant. The analysis for the directed variant is analogous.

We present an existence proof based on the randomized rounding technique. It can be derandomized by the method of pairwise independence. The difficulty in applying this technique to the interference scheduling problem is the non-convex domain of this problem. We circumvent this difficulty by considering the requests from a fixed color class of c for given power assignment

3. Oblivious Power Assignments and the Bidirectional Model

p.

Proposition 3.2.2. *Let S denote a set of requests with power assignment p satisfying the SINR constraints with threshold β. Then there exists a subset S' of S with $|S'| \geq \beta/8\beta'|S|$ satisfying the SINR constraints with threshold $\beta' > \beta$ for the same power assignment.*

Proof. Suppose every request from S is chosen with probability $\beta/4\beta'$. To simplify notation, we identify requests (u_i, v_i) with their index i. For $i \in S$, let X_i be a random variable such that $X_i = 1$ if request i is chosen and 0, otherwise. We assume that the X_i's are pairwise independent. Let $S'' = \{i \in S \mid X_i = 1\}$.

Consider a request $i = (u_i, v_i)$. It holds $\mathbf{Pr}\left[X_i = 1\right] = \beta/4\beta'$. Let us have a closer look at the interference at u_i conditioning on $X_i = 1$. For $j \neq i$, let

$$w_j = \frac{p_j}{\min\{d(u_j, u_i)^\alpha, d(v_j, u_i)^\alpha\}} \cdot \frac{d(u_i, v_i)^\alpha}{p_i} ,$$

that is, w_j is the normalized strength of the signals from (u_j, v_j) received at u_i. As S satisfies the SINR constraints with threshold β, it holds $\sum_{j \in S \setminus \{i\}} w_j \leq \beta^{-1}$. Let the normalized interference at u_i under S'' be defined by

$$W(u_i) = \sum_{j \in S'' \setminus \{i\}} w_j .$$

By linearity of expectation,

$$\mathbf{E}\left[W(u_i) \mid X_i = 1\right] = \sum_{j \in S \setminus \{i\}} w_j \, \mathbf{E}\left[X_j \mid X_i = 1\right] .$$

Observe that $\mathbf{E}\left[X_j \mid X_i = 1\right] = \mathbf{Pr}\left[X_j = 1 \mid X_i = 1\right] = \frac{\beta}{4\beta'}$ because of pairwise independence. Consequently,

$$\mathbf{E}\left[W(u_i) \mid X_i = 1\right] = \frac{\beta}{4\beta'} \sum_{j \in S \setminus \{i\}} w_j \leq \frac{1}{4\beta'} .$$

Now applying the Markov inequality gives

$$\mathbf{Pr}\left[W(u_i) \geq \beta'^{-1} \mid X_i = 1\right] \leq \frac{1}{4} .$$

3.2 The Square Root Assignment

The same is true for $W(v_i)$. Thus, the probability that request i violates the SINR constraint with threshold β' is at most

$$\mathbf{Pr}\left[W(u_i) \geq \beta'^{-1} \vee W(v_i) \geq \beta'^{-1} \mid X_i = 1\right] \leq \frac{1}{2}.$$

Now let S' be the set of those requests from S''' that satisfy the SINR constraints with threshold β'. Our analysis above shows that the probability that a request i from S is contained in S' is $\mathbf{Pr}\left[X_i = 1\right] \cdot \mathbf{Pr}\left[i \in S' | X_i = 1\right] \geq \beta/4\beta' \cdot 1/2 = \beta/8\beta'$. Hence, by linearity of expectation, the expected cardinality of S' is at least $\beta/8\beta'|S|$. □

Let us remark that the randomized existence proof above can be made constructive by applying the derandomization technique of pairwise independence. This yields a deterministic polynomial time algorithm for computing a set of requests $|S'|$ of cardinality, say, $\beta/9\beta'|S|$ instead of $\beta/8\beta'|S|$.

We are now ready to prove the following

Proposition 3.2.3. *Let S denote a set of requests with power assignment p satisfying the SINR constraints with threshold β. Then there exists a coloring c' for S with $\mathcal{O}(\beta/\beta' \log |S|)$ colors such that c' together with p satisfy the SINR constraints with threshold $\beta' > \beta$.*

Proof. Choose a subset S' from S with $|S'| \geq |S|\beta/8\beta'$ and assign the first color to the requests in S'. The remaining subset of size at most $|S| \cdot (1 - \beta/8\beta')$ is colored recursively. This yields a coloring with at most $-\log|S|/\log(1 - \beta/8\beta') + 1 = \mathcal{O}(\beta/\beta' \log|S|)$ colors. □

3.2.2 Splitting Pairs

For our analysis of the interference scheduling problem we use a slightly modified variant, the *node-loss scheduling problem*. One is given a set of nodes $[n]$ and each node i is associated with a *loss parameter* ℓ_i. For every $i \in [n] := \{1, \ldots, n\}$, one needs to specify a power level $p_i > 0$ and a color $c_i \in [k] := \{1, \ldots, k\}$ such that the number of colors, k, is minimized and the pairs in each color class satisfy the following *SINR constraints*.

$$\frac{p_i}{\ell_i} \geq \beta \left(\sum_{\substack{j \in [n] \setminus \{i\} \\ c_j = c_i}} \frac{p_j}{d(i,j)^\alpha} + N \right)$$

3. Oblivious Power Assignments and the Bidirectional Model

In words, for each node the ratio between the power p_i and the loss ℓ_i needs to be at least β times larger than the sum of the strengths of the signals sent by other nodes plus the noise. Again we neglect the ambient noise in the model, i.e., $N = 0$ and fulfill the SINR constraints with ">" rather than "$\geq$".

A *power assignment* specifies a power level for each node. The *square root power assignment* $\bar{p}$ sets the power level for node $i \in [n]$ equal to $\sqrt{\ell_i}$. For a power assignment $p = p_1, \ldots, p_n$ and a set of nodes $U \subseteq [n]$, let

$$I_p(i \mid U) = \sum_{j \in U \setminus \{i\}} \frac{p_j}{d(i,j)^\alpha}$$

denote the *interference* at node $i \in [n]$ induced by elements of U. We say that U is β-*feasible* for a power assignment p if $\frac{p_i}{\ell_i} > \beta I_p(i \mid U)$, for every $i \in U$.

On any given instance, feasible schedule steps for the interference scheduling and the node-loss scheduling problem are related as follows: First, if we have a feasible schedule step S for the node-loss scheduling that schedules a fraction greater than one half of the nodes, we can give a feasible schedule step for a constant fraction of the nodes in the interference scheduling setting by scheduling the pairs with both nodes in S.

Second, if we have a set of pairs U that we can schedule in the interference scheduling setting with SINR threshold β, the set of all nodes from pairs in U is $\beta/{2+\beta}$-feasible for the node-loss scenario, as we show in the following. For a node i let $I'(i)$ denote the interference at this node in the interference scheduling problem, and $I(i)$ denote the interference at this node in the node-loss scheduling problem. If now all nodes from pairs in U transmit, the interference at a single node i is at most twice the interference from the interference scheduling problem plus the interference from the other node of this pair, i.e., p_i/ℓ_i, so

$$I(i) \leq 2I'(i) + \frac{p_i}{\ell_i} \leq \frac{2+\beta}{\beta} \cdot \frac{p_i}{\ell_i},$$

as $I'(i) \leq p_i/\beta\ell_i$. As the results from Section 3.2.1 can be proven analogously for the node-loss scheduling problem, we can compute a schedule for the node-loss scheduling problem from a schedule for the interference scheduling problem, that is longer by at most a logarithmic factor.

3.2 The Square Root Assignment

In Section 3.2.6 we prove for the node-loss scheduling problem the following result.

Lemma 3.2.4. *Let $\beta' \geq \beta > 0$. Suppose $S([n], d, \ell)$ is a star for which there exists a power assignment p such that $[n]$ is β'-feasible under p. Then there is a subset $U \subseteq [n]$ with $|U| \geq (1 - \mathcal{O}((\frac{\beta}{\beta'})^{2/3})))n$ that is β-feasible under the square root assignment $\bar{p}$.*

There a star $S([n], d, \ell)$ is defined by a set $[n]$ of nodes placed around a center c, the distances of the nodes d and their loss parameters ℓ (see Section 3.2.6 for details). Using this lemma we now turn to the proof for Theorem 3.2.1.

3.2.3 From General Metrics to Trees

For this part we utilize the following lemma, which is suitably adapted from a lemma in [GHR06].

Lemma 3.2.5. *Given a finite metric space $([n], d)$ there exist $r = \mathcal{O}(\log n)$ edge-weighted trees $T_1, \ldots, T_r$ with node-set $[n]$ such that the following holds*

1. *For every pair $(u, v) \in [n]^2$ and for every tree T_i: $d(u, v) \leq d_{T_i}(u, v)$ where d_{T_i} denotes the shortest path metric induced by tree T_i.*

2. *For every node $v \in [n]$ there exists a subset $\mathcal{T}_v \subseteq \{T_1, \ldots, T_r\}$ with $|\mathcal{T}_v| \geq \frac{9}{10} r$ such that the pairwise distances involving v are stretched by at most a logarithmic factor, i.e., $\forall T \in \mathcal{T}_v : \forall u \in [n] : d_T(u, v) \leq \mathcal{O}(\log n) \cdot d(u, v)$.*

For a tree T_i in the above lemma we call the set of nodes whose distances are at most stretched by the logarithmic factor the *core of* T_i, and denote it with C_i. Suppose that we are given an instance of the node-loss scheduling problem in a metric space $([n], d)$. With every tree T_i from the decomposition of Lemma 3.2.5 we associate a corresponding node-loss scheduling instance that only includes nodes in the core of T_i (the loss parameters stay the same).

Proposition 3.2.6. *Suppose there exists a β'-feasible set $U \subseteq [n]$ for the node-loss scheduling problem on $([n], d)$. Then there exists a tree T_i with a β'-feasible set of size at least $\frac{9}{10} \cdot |U|$ in its core C_i.*

3. Oblivious Power Assignments and the Bidirectional Model

Proof. Since the distances in a tree increase, any set that is β'-feasible w.r.t. the original metric is still feasible in a tree. Let $j^* := \arg\max_j |U \cap C_j|$ and define $U' := U \cap C_{j^*}$. Note that $\sum_i |U \cap C_i| \geq \frac{9}{10}|U|r$ as every node in U is in the core of at least $\frac{9}{10}r$ trees. Hence, $|U'| \geq \frac{9}{10}|U|$ and T_{j^*} is the desired tree. □

Lemma 3.2.7. *Suppose there is a β'-feasible subset U of core nodes for the node-loss scheduling instance in a tree T_i (for some power assignment p). Then, this set U is β''-feasible with respect to the original metric for $\beta'' = \Omega(\frac{\beta'}{\log^\alpha n})$.*

Proof. For nodes in the core the distances to other nodes decrease by at most a logarithmic factor $f = \mathcal{O}(\log n)$, when going from the tree distance to the original distance. This in turn can only increase the interference at a node by a factor of f^α. This means that for every node $i \in U$, the inequality $p_i/\ell_i > \beta' I_p(i \mid U)$ implies $p_i/\ell_i > \frac{\beta'}{f^\alpha}I'_p(i \mid U)$, where $I_p(i \mid U)$ and $I'_p(i \mid U)$ denote the interference in the tree metric and the original metric, respectively. □

3.2.4 From Trees to Stars

In this section we extend Lemma 3.2.4 to tree metrics.

Lemma 3.2.8. *Suppose we are given an instance $T([n], d, \ell)$ of the node-loss scheduling problem on a tree metric for which there exists a power assignment p such that a subset $U \subseteq [n]$ is β'-feasible under p. Then, there exists a subset $U' \subseteq U$ with $|U'| \geq \frac{9}{10}|U|$ that is β-feasible under $\bar{p}$ for $\beta = \Omega(\frac{\beta'}{\log^{2.5} n})$.*

Proof. In order to show the result we repeatedly make use of Lemma 3.2.4, and remove nodes from the set U that cannot be scheduled by the square root power assignment in one round. In the end we show that we did not remove too many nodes from U. For the first round we choose a node c in the tree such that the removal of c partitions the tree into disjoint sub-trees with size at most $n/2$. Such a node can be found in any tree. Now we consider the node-loss scheduling problem on the star metric obtained by selecting c as center and setting the distance d_v of a node v to the center as the tree-distance $d(v, c)$. Note that distances in this star-metric are not smaller than distances in the original tree and that therefore the set U is β'-feasible in this metric.

3.2 The Square Root Assignment

When applying Lemma 3.2.4 with a suitable parameter $\beta'' = \beta/\mathcal{O}(\log^{3/2} n)$ we obtain a subset $U_1' \subset U$, $|U_1'| \geq (1 - \frac{1}{10 \log n})|U|$ that is β''-feasible for the square root power assignment $\bar{p}$. Here the constant 10 comes from suitably balancing the hidden constant in the $\mathcal{O}$-notation of Lemma 3.2.4 and the hidden constant in the $\mathcal{O}$-notation of β''. Of course, this subset may not be feasible for the square root power assignment in the original tree metric $([n], d)$, because some nodes of U_1' are closer in $([n], d)$ and hence induce more interference between each other. In order to compensate for this we re-run the algorithm on the forest obtained after splitting the graph at c, i.e., we delete all but one edge incident to c. In each of the trees of this forest we run the above algorithm recursively. For each level i of the recursion, the algorithm returns a set U_i', $|U_i'| \geq (1 - \frac{1}{10 \log n})|U|$ that is β''-feasible in the corresponding forest. There are at most $\log n$ recursion levels as the size of a tree reduces by at least a factor of 2 in each iteration. Let $U' := \bigcap_i U_i'$. Then we have $|U'| \geq 9|U|/10$.

Note that a pair $(u, v) \in U' \times U'$ has the correct distance in at least one of the recursions. Therefore, the total interference induced at a node $u \in U'$ (from all the other nodes of U') when using the square root assignment in the tree metric $([n], d)$ is at most the sum of the interferences generated at u in all iterations which is at most $\log n \cdot \frac{1}{\beta''\sqrt{\ell_u}}$, since u is β''-feasible in each iteration. This means that the set U' is $\beta = \frac{\beta''}{\log n} = \Omega(\frac{\beta'}{\log^{2.5} n})$-feasible. $\square$

3.2.5 Putting the Pieces Together

In this section we prove Theorem 3.2.1.

- We are given a set S of request pairs from a metric space $([n], d)$ for which there is a power assignment that is feasible for bidirectional SINR constraints within a single schedule step. Let U denote the set of terminal nodes of pairs from S. Following the discussion in Section 3.2.2 this set is β'-feasible for the node-loss scheduling problem with $\beta' \geq \frac{\beta}{2+\beta}$ (on the same metric $([n], d)$).

- We apply Proposition 3.2.6 to this set U, and obtain a subset $U' \subset U$, $|U'| \geq \frac{9}{10}|U|$ that is β'-feasible and is contained in the core C_i of a tree T_i.

- We apply Lemma 3.2.8 to this set and obtain a subset U'', $|U''| \geq$

49

3. Oblivious Power Assignments and the Bidirectional Model

$\frac{9}{10}|U'|$ that is β''-feasible for the square root assignment $\bar{p}$, where $\beta'' = \Omega(\beta'/\log^{2.5} n)$.

- Lemma 3.2.7 gives that this set is also β'''-feasible for $\bar{p}$ in the original metric, where $\beta''' = \Omega(\beta''/\log^\alpha n)$.

- Note that the subset U'' contains at least $\frac{9}{10} \cdot \frac{9}{10}|U| > \frac{8}{10}|U|$ nodes. This means that for at least a $\frac{6}{10}$-fraction of pairs from the original set S, both end-points are contained in U''. Let $S' \subset S$ denote a set that contains only these pairs. The pairs in S' fulfill the bidirectional SINR constraints with threshold β''' for the power assignment $\bar{p}$.

- Rescaling the SINR threshold with Proposition 3.2.2, we obtain a subset S'' with $|S''| \geq \beta'''/8\beta$ that fulfills the SINR constraints with threshold β.

- Observe that the size of S'' is $\Omega(1/\beta \log^{2.5+\alpha} n)|S|$. Assigning the requests from S'' to one schedule step and repeating the process for the remaining request gives that we get a schedule of length $\mathcal{O}(\log^{3.5+\alpha} n)$.

This completes the proof of the theorem.

3.2.6 Analysis for Star Metrics

In this Section, we prove Lemma 3.2.4. Let $\beta' \geq \beta > 0$. We are given a set $\{(1, \ell_1), \ldots, (n, \ell_n)\}$ of node-loss pairs (requests) being β'-feasible under some power assignment p. The nodes $1, \ldots, n$ form a star centered around an additional node c. The distance between c and i is denoted by d_i. Let $\delta_i = d_i^\alpha$, that is, δ_i corresponds to the loss between c and i. In the following, this parameter is called *decay* in order to distinguish it from the loss parameter ℓ_i. W.l.o.g., we assume $\delta_1 \leq \delta_2 \leq \cdots \leq \delta_n$. Let $a_i = \ell_i/\delta_i$. We have to show that there exists a subset $U \subseteq [n]$ with $|U| \geq (1 - \mathcal{O}((\frac{\beta}{\beta'})^{2/3}))n$ being β-feasible under the square root power assignment $\bar{p}$.

We will first prove some helpful properties. These properties will show that the lemma follows relatively easy for the special case in which the loss parameter is relatively large in comparison to the decay, i.e., $a_i > 2^{\alpha+1}/\beta'$, for every $i \in [n]$. We then turn our attention to the case in which the loss parameter is relatively small, i.e. $a_i \leq 2^{\alpha+1}/\beta'$, for every $i \in [n]$. Finally, we will combine the results for these special cases in order to prove the lemma for stars with both small and large loss parameters.

3.2 The Square Root Assignment

Helpful properties

Consider two nodes i and i' with $i' < i$. As there exists a power scheme p with a β'-feasible schedule, it holds that

$$\frac{p_{i'}}{\ell_{i'}} > \beta' \frac{p_i}{(d_i + d_{i'})^\alpha} \quad \text{and} \quad \frac{p_i}{\ell_i} > \beta' \frac{p_{i'}}{(d_i + d_{i'})^\alpha} \ .$$

Multiplying these equations we obtain $(d_i + d_{i'})^{2\alpha} > \beta'^2 \cdot \ell_i \cdot \ell_{i'}$. As $i' < i$ we have $(2d_i)^{2\alpha} \geq (d_i + d_{i'})^{2\alpha}$ and thus

$$\delta_i^2 = d_i^{2\alpha} > \frac{\beta'^2}{4^\alpha} \cdot \ell_i \cdot \ell_{i'} \ . \tag{3.1}$$

It follows

$$\delta_i \geq a_i \cdot \frac{\beta'^2}{4^\alpha} \cdot \ell_{i'} \ , \tag{3.2}$$

$$\delta_i \geq a_i \cdot a_{i'} \cdot \frac{\beta'^2}{4^\alpha} \cdot \delta_{i'} \ , \tag{3.3}$$

$$\ell_i \geq a_i^2 \cdot \frac{\beta'^2}{4^\alpha} \cdot \ell_{i'} \ . \tag{3.4}$$

Stars with large loss parameters

In this section, we assume $a_i > {}^{2^{\alpha+1}}\!/_{\beta'}$, for every $i \in [n]$. We apply Equation 3.4 with $\ell_{i'} = \ell_{i-1}$ and repeat this for $i - j$ times deriving the following lower bound relating ℓ_i to ℓ_j, for $i > j$,

$$\begin{aligned}
\ell_i &\geq a_i^2 \cdot \ldots \cdot a_{j+1}^2 \cdot \ell_j \cdot \left(\frac{\beta'}{2^\alpha}\right)^{2(i-j)} \\
&> a_i^2 \cdot \left(\frac{2^{\alpha+1}}{\beta'}\right)^{2(i-j-1)} \cdot \ell_j \cdot \left(\frac{\beta'}{2^\alpha}\right)^{2(i-j)} \\
&= a_i^2 \cdot \left(\frac{\beta'}{2^{\alpha+1}}\right)^2 \cdot \ell_j \cdot 2^{2(i-j)} \ .
\end{aligned} \tag{3.5}$$

Now we solve the equation above for ℓ_j and exchange the indices i and j. This way, for $i < j$,

$$\ell_i < a_j^{-2} \cdot \left(\frac{2^{\alpha+1}}{\beta'}\right)^2 \cdot \ell_j \cdot 2^{2(i-j)} \ . \tag{3.6}$$

3. Oblivious Power Assignments and the Bidirectional Model

These inequalities enable us to prove the following result for stars with large loss parameters.

Lemma 3.2.9. *Suppose $a_i > 2^{\alpha+1}/\beta'$, for every $i \in [n]$. If there exists a power scheme p such that $[n]$ is β'-feasible under p then $[n]$ is β-feasible under the square root power assignment $\bar{p}$ with $\beta \leq \beta'/2^{\alpha+2}$.*

Proof. At node j the received interference is

$$I_{\bar{p}}(j) \leq \sum_{i=1}^{j-1} \frac{\sqrt{\ell_i}}{\delta_j} + \sum_{i=j+1}^{n} \frac{\sqrt{\ell_i}}{\delta_i} = \sum_{i=1}^{j-1} \frac{\sqrt{\ell_i}}{\delta_j} + \sum_{i=j+1}^{n} \frac{a_i}{\sqrt{\ell_i}}.$$

Now applying Equation 3.6 and Equation 3.5 gives

$$I_{\bar{p}}(j) < \frac{\sqrt{\ell_j}}{a_j \delta_j} \cdot \frac{2^{\alpha+1}}{\beta'} \cdot \sum_{i=1}^{j-1} 2^{i-j} + \frac{1}{\sqrt{\ell_j}} \cdot \frac{2^{\alpha+1}}{\beta'} \cdot \sum_{i=j+1}^{n} 2^{j-i} < \frac{2}{\sqrt{\ell_j}} \cdot \frac{2^{\alpha+1}}{\beta'}.$$

The SINR constraint at j is satisfied if $I_{\bar{p}}(j) < 1/\beta\sqrt{\ell_i}$. For $\beta \leq \beta'/2^{\alpha+2}$ this condition is satisfied. □

Stars with small loss parameters

Now we assume that all loss parameters are relatively large in comparison to the decay. In this case, given a β'-feasible power assignment p, we can ensure that the square root power assignment is β-feasible for any $\beta < \beta'$ if a small fraction of the nodes that depends on the ratio between β and β' can be dropped.

Lemma 3.2.10. *Suppose $a_i \leq 2^{\alpha+1}/\beta'$, for every $i \in [n]$. If there exists a power scheme p such that $[n]$ is β'-feasible under p then there exists a subset $U \subseteq [n]$ that is β-feasible under $\bar{p}$ with $|U| = (1 - \mathcal{O}((\frac{\beta}{\beta'})^{2/3}))n$.*

Proof. We partition the nodes into classes depending on their distance/decay to the center c. W.l.o.g., assume $\delta_u > 1$, for every $u \in [n]$. Let $D_j = \{u \mid 2^{j-1} < \delta_u \leq 2^j\}, |D_j| = k_j$ and let m denote the largest index for which D_m is not empty.

Claim 3.2.11. *Let $0 < \mu < 1$. For a $(1-\mu)$-fraction of the nodes in class D_j, the loss parameter ℓ_u fulfills $\ell_u \leq \frac{2^{\alpha+j+2}}{\mu\beta' k_j}$.*

3.2 The Square Root Assignment

Proof. In the given power assignment p, a node v from class D_j induces an interference on node $u \in D_j$ of

$$\frac{p_v}{(d_u + d_v)^\alpha} \geq \frac{p_v}{(2 \cdot 2^{j/\alpha})^\alpha} = \frac{p_v}{2^{\alpha+j}} \ .$$

The interference at node u is upper-bounded by $p_u/\beta'\ell_u$ because p satisfies the SINR constraint. Thus, it follows

$$\sum_{v \in D_j \setminus \{u\}} \frac{p_v}{2^{\alpha+j}} \leq \sum_{v \in [n] \setminus \{u\}} \frac{p_v}{d(u,v)^\alpha} \leq \frac{p_u}{\beta'\ell_u} \ .$$

For nodes u that fulfill $p_u \leq \sum_{v \in D_j \setminus \{u\}} p_v$, we thus get

$$\ell_u \leq \frac{2^{\alpha+j}}{\beta'} \cdot \frac{p_u}{\sum_{v \in D_j \setminus \{u\}} p_v} \leq \frac{2^{\alpha+j+1}}{\beta'} \cdot \frac{p_u}{\sum_{v \in D_j} p_v} \ .$$

For the other nodes,

$$\ell_u \leq a_u \cdot \delta_u \leq \frac{2^{\alpha+j+1}}{\beta'} \leq \frac{2^{\alpha+j+2}}{\beta'} \cdot \frac{p_u}{\sum_{v \in D_j} p_v}$$

since $p_u > \sum_{v \in D_j \setminus \{u\}} p_v$ implies $2p_u > \sum_{v \in D_j} p_v$. Summing the above inequality over all nodes in the class D_j gives

$$\sum_{u \in D_j} \ell_u \leq \frac{2^{\alpha+j+2}}{\beta'} \ .$$

This means that, on average, a node has a loss parameter of only $2^{\alpha+j+2}/(\beta'k_j)$. Using the Markov inequality, we get that a fraction of at most μ of the nodes have a loss parameter larger than $2^{\alpha+j+2}/(\mu\beta'k_j)$. □

Claim 3.2.11 is based on properties of p. In the remainder of the proof of Lemma 3.2.10, we will not consider other properties of p than the one given by the claim. For the time being, let us ignore a μ-fraction of the nodes such that all remaining nodes fulfill the bound in the claim. The μ-fraction dropped will be taken into account at the end of the proof of the lemma.

When using the square root power assignment, the interference induced

3. Oblivious Power Assignments and the Bidirectional Model

at a node $u \in D_j$ by a node $v \in D_i$, $i \leq j$ is at most

$$\frac{\sqrt{\ell_v}}{2^{j-1}} \leq \frac{1}{2^{j-1}}\sqrt{\frac{2^{\alpha+i+2}}{\mu\beta'k_i}} = \frac{1}{2^j}\sqrt{\frac{2^{\alpha+i+4}}{\mu\beta'k_i}} .$$

Summing this over all nodes in the class and then over all classes gives the following bound on the interference generated at u by nodes from classes with lower or equal index:

$$I_{\bar{p}}(u \mid D_1 \cup \ldots \cup D_j) \leq \sqrt{\frac{2^{\alpha+4}}{\mu\beta'}} \sum_{i=1}^{j} \frac{\sqrt{k_i 2^i}}{2^j} .$$

The interference generated by nodes from higher classes can be estimated as

$$I_{\bar{p}}(u \mid D_{j+1} \cup \ldots \cup D_m) \leq \sqrt{\frac{2^{\alpha+4}}{\mu\beta'}} \sum_{i=j+1}^{m} \frac{\sqrt{k_i 2^i}}{2^i} .$$

We now select all nodes for which, both, the interference from classes with lower index and the interference from classes with higher index, is no more than $1/2\beta$ times the strength of the received signal.

We first count the number of nodes that are not selected this way because the interference from classes with lower or equal index is too high, that is, the number of nodes $u \in D_j$ satisfying

$$I_{\bar{p}}(u \mid D_1 \cup \ldots \cup D_j) \geq \frac{1}{2\beta} \frac{1}{\sqrt{\ell_u}} \geq \frac{1}{2\beta}\sqrt{\frac{\mu\beta'k_j}{2^{\alpha+j+2}}}$$

as the received signal strength at a node u in class D_j is

$$\frac{\sqrt{\ell_u}}{\ell_u} \geq \sqrt{\frac{\mu\beta'k_j}{2^{\alpha+j+2}}} .$$

Together with the above bound on the interference we obtain

$$k_j \leq \left(\frac{2^{\alpha+4}\beta}{\mu\beta'}\right)^2 \left(\sum_{i=1}^{j}\sqrt{\frac{k_i}{2^{j-i}}}\right)^2$$

3.2 The Square Root Assignment

$$= \left(\frac{2^{\alpha+4}\beta}{\mu\beta'}\right)^2 \left(\sum_{i=1}^{j} \sqrt{\frac{k_i}{\sqrt{2^{j-i}}}} \cdot \sqrt{\frac{1}{\sqrt{2^{j-i}}}}\right)^2$$

$$\leq \left(\frac{2^{\alpha+4}\beta}{\mu\beta'}\right)^2 \left(\sum_{i=1}^{j} \frac{k_i}{\sqrt{2^{j-i}}}\right) \cdot \left(\sum_{i=1}^{j} \frac{1}{\sqrt{2^{j-i}}}\right)$$

$$\leq \left(\frac{2^{\alpha+6}\beta}{\mu\beta'}\right)^2 \sum_{i=1}^{j} \frac{k_i}{\sqrt{2^{j-i}}} \ .$$

Here the third inequality uses Cauchy-Schwarz $((\sum a_i b_i)^2 \leq \sum a_i^2 \cdot \sum b_i^2)$. Now the number of nodes lost because of too much interference from classes with lower or equal index can be estimated by

$$\sum_{\substack{j\,:\,\text{class } D_j \\ \text{not scheduled}}} k_j \leq \sum_{j=1}^{m} \left(\frac{2^{\alpha+6}\beta}{\mu\beta'}\right)^2 \sum_{i=1}^{j} \frac{k_i}{\sqrt{2^{j-i}}}$$

$$= \left(\frac{2^{\alpha+6}\beta}{\mu\beta'}\right)^2 \sum_{i=1}^{m} k_i \sum_{j=i}^{m} \frac{1}{\sqrt{2^{j-i}}}$$

$$\leq \left(\frac{2^{\alpha+8}\beta}{\mu\beta'}\right)^2 \sum_{i=1}^{m} k_i \ .$$

Analogously the number of nodes lost because of too much interference from classes with higher index is at most

$$\sum_{\substack{j\colon\text{class } D_j \\ \text{not scheduled}}} k_j \leq \sum_{j=1}^{m-1} \left(\frac{2^{\alpha+6}\beta}{\mu\beta'}\right)^2 \sum_{i=j+1}^{m} \frac{k_i}{\sqrt{2^{i-j}}}$$

$$\leq \left(\frac{2^{\alpha+6}\beta}{\mu\beta'}\right)^2 \sum_{i=2}^{m} \sum_{j=1}^{i-1} \frac{k_i}{\sqrt{2^{i-j}}}$$

$$\leq \left(\frac{2^{\alpha+8}\beta}{\mu\beta'}\right)^2 \sum_{i=2}^{m} k_i \ .$$

So in total we only lose $\mathcal{O}((\frac{\beta}{\mu\beta'})^2 + \mu)n$ nodes. Choosing $\mu = (\frac{\beta}{\beta'})^{2/3}$ gives the bound in Lemma 3.2.10. □

3. Oblivious Power Assignments and the Bidirectional Model

Stars with arbitrary combinations of loss parameters

In the following, we use the results for the special cases given in Lemma 3.2.9 and Lemma 3.2.10 to prove Lemma 3.2.4 for stars without any restrictions on the ratio a_i between ℓ_i and δ_i.

W.l.o.g., assume that $\beta' \geq 2c_0\beta$ and choose $\beta'' = 2c_1\beta$, for suitable large positive constant terms c_0 and c_1 as specified at the end of the proof. We will show that there is a way to remove a subset of $\Theta((\beta''/\beta')^{2/3})n = \Theta((\beta/\beta')^{2/3})n$ many nodes such that the interference at any remaining node i is at most $(c_0/\beta' + c_1/\beta'') \cdot 1/\sqrt{\ell_i} \leq 1/\beta\sqrt{\ell_i}$, that is, the set of the remaining nodes is β-feasible.

Suppose we hypothetically reduce the loss ℓ_i, for every $i \in [n]$ with $\ell_i > \delta_i \cdot 2^{\alpha+1}/\beta'$, to $\delta_i \cdot 2^{\alpha+1}/\beta'$. Under this hypothesis, all nodes have small loss parameters so that Lemma 3.2.10 shows the existence of a subset $U \subseteq [n]$ that is β''-feasible (with respect to the hypothetical loss parameters) under $\bar{p}$ with $|U| = (1 - \mathcal{O}((\frac{\beta''}{\beta'})^{2/3}))n$. In the following, we will study the interference caused by the square root power assignment applied to the nodes in U with respect to the original loss parameters.

Define the set $L \subseteq U$ of *large loss nodes* by $L := \{i \in [n] \mid a_i > 2^{\alpha+1}/\beta'\}$. For a node $i \in U$, we use $\text{pred}(i) := \max\{j \in L \mid j < i\}$ and $\text{succ}(i) := \min\{j \in L \mid j > i\}$ to denote the predecessor and successor, respectively, of i in L. The nodes in L partition the remaining nodes into subsets as follows. For $i \in L$ we define the set $S_i := \{j \in U \mid \text{pred}(i) < j < i\}$.

The interference that is induced by *large-loss nodes* (nodes in L) onto other large-loss nodes can be handled by applying Lemma 3.2.9. Similarly, the interference that is induced by *low-loss nodes* (nodes not in L) onto other low-loss nodes can be handled by Lemma 3.2.10. In the following two lemmas we will derive bounds for the interference that is induced by small-loss nodes onto large-loss nodes and vice versa.

Lemma 3.2.12. *For every node* $i \in L$,

$$\sum_{j \in L \setminus \{i, \text{succ}(i)\}} I_{\bar{p}}(i \mid S_j) < \frac{2^\alpha}{\beta'' \sqrt{\ell_i}} \ .$$

In words, for a node $i \in L$, the interference generated at i by the small-loss nodes in the sets S_j (with exception of S_i and $S_{\text{succ}(i)}$), is less than $1/\sqrt{\ell_i}$, the strength of the signal received at node i, times $2^\alpha/\beta''$.

Proof. To show the lemma, we split the interference at i from classes S_j into

3.2 The Square Root Assignment

two parts, the interference from classes $S_j, j \in L, j < i$, and interference from classes $S_j, j \in L, j > \text{succ}(i)$. We will show that each of these terms is upper-bounded by $2^\alpha/2\beta''\sqrt{\ell_i}$, which proves the lemma.

The interference at node i due to the classes $S_j, j \in L, j < i$ can be bounded as follows. We first prove an upper bound on the interference at node $\text{pred}(i)$ and then we show that this bound translates to the desired upper bound for the interference at node i. Let $L^{<i} := \{j \in L \mid j < i\}$. The interference at node $\text{pred}(i)$ from sets $S_j, j \in L^{<i}$ is at least

$$\sum_{j \in L^{<i}} \sum_{k \in S_j} \frac{\sqrt{\ell_k}}{(d_k + d_{\text{pred}(i)})^\alpha} \geq \sum_{j \in L^{<i}} \sum_{k \in S_j} \frac{\sqrt{\ell_k}}{(2 \cdot d_{\text{pred}(i)})^\alpha} = \sum_{j \in L^{<i}} \sum_{k \in S_j} \frac{\sqrt{\ell_k}}{2^\alpha \delta_{\text{pred}(i)}}.$$

For every $j \in U$, let $\ell'_j = \delta_j \cdot a'_j$ with $a'_j = \min\{a_j, 2^{\alpha+1}/\beta'\}$, that is, we decrease the large loss parameters so that all loss parameters $\ell'_j, j \in U$, are small. On the one hand, due to the construction of the set U, the interference at node $\text{pred}(i)$ caused by the nodes from U wrt to the loss parameters ℓ'_j is upper-bounded by $1/\beta'' \sqrt{\ell'_{\text{pred}(i)}}$ because the nodes in U are β''-feasible wrt modified loss parameters. On the other hand, the lower bound on the interference at $\text{pred}(i)$ is valid also for the modified loss parameters as it only sums over the strengths of signals received from nodes with small loss parameters. Consequently,

$$\sum_{j \in L^{<i}} \sum_{k \in S_j} \frac{\sqrt{\ell_k}}{2^\alpha \delta_{\text{pred}(i)}} \leq \frac{1}{\beta'' \sqrt{\ell'_{\text{pred}(i)}}} = \frac{1}{\beta'' \sqrt{a'_{\text{pred}(i)} \delta_{\text{pred}(i)}}}.$$

By multiplying with $\delta_{\text{pred}(i)} 2^\alpha / \delta_i$, we get

$$\sum_{j \in L^{<i}} \sum_{k \in S_j} \frac{\sqrt{\ell_k}}{\delta_i} \leq \frac{2^\alpha \sqrt{\delta_{\text{pred}(i)}}}{\beta'' \delta_i \sqrt{a'_{\text{pred}(i)}}} < \frac{4^\alpha}{\beta' \beta'' a'_{\text{pred}(i)} \sqrt{a_i \delta_i}} = \frac{2^\alpha}{2\beta'' \sqrt{\ell_i}},$$

where we used $\delta_{\text{pred}(i)} \leq \frac{4^\alpha}{\beta'^2} \frac{\delta_i}{a_i a_{\text{pred}(i)}} < \frac{4^\alpha}{\beta'^2} \frac{\delta_i}{a_i a'_{\text{pred}(i)}}$ (Equation 3.3) for the second step and the identities $a'_{\text{pred}(i)} = 2^{\alpha+1}/\beta'$ and $a_i \delta_i = \ell_i$ for the last one. Now observe that the left hand term of this equation is an upper bound on the interference at node i due to the classes $S_j, j \in L^{<i}$ such that the desired bound on this interference is shown.

Next we show that the interference at node i due to the classes $S_j, j \in$

3. Oblivious Power Assignments and the Bidirectional Model

$L, j < i$ can be bounded by a similar approach studying the interference at $\operatorname{succ}(i)$ instead of $\operatorname{pred}(i)$. Let $L^{>\operatorname{succ}(i)} := \{j \in L \mid j > \operatorname{succ}(i)\}$. The interference at node $\operatorname{succ}(i)$ from sets S_j, $j \in L^{>\operatorname{succ}(i)}$ is

$$\sum_{j \in L^{>\operatorname{succ}(i)}} \sum_{k \in S_j} \frac{\sqrt{\ell_k}}{(d_k + d_{\operatorname{succ}(i)})^\alpha} \geq \sum_{j \in L^{>\operatorname{succ}(i)}} \sum_{k \in S_j} \frac{\sqrt{\ell_k}}{(2 \cdot d_k)^\alpha}$$

$$= \sum_{j \in L^{>\operatorname{succ}(i)}} \sum_{k \in S_j} \frac{\sqrt{\ell_k}}{2^\alpha \delta_k} \; .$$

Analogously to the case above, the interference at node $\operatorname{succ}(i)$ due to the nodes from U wrt to the loss parameters ℓ'_j is upper-bounded by $1/\beta'' \sqrt{\ell'_{\operatorname{pred}(i)}}$ so that

$$\sum_{j \in L^{>\operatorname{succ}(i)}} \sum_{k \in S_j} \frac{\sqrt{\ell_k}}{2^\alpha \delta_k} \leq \frac{1}{\beta'' \sqrt{\ell'_{\operatorname{succ}(i)}}} = \frac{1}{\beta'' \sqrt{a'_{\operatorname{succ}(i)} \delta_{\operatorname{succ}(i)}}} \; .$$

By multiplying with 2^α, we get

$$\sum_{j \in L^{<i}} \sum_{k \in S_j} \frac{\sqrt{\ell_k}}{\delta_k} \leq \frac{2^\alpha}{\beta'' \sqrt{a'_{\operatorname{succ}(i)} \delta_{\operatorname{succ}(i)}}} < \frac{4^\alpha}{\beta' \beta'' a'_{\operatorname{succ}(i)} \sqrt{a_i \delta_i}} = \frac{2^\alpha}{2\beta'' \sqrt{\ell_i}} \; ,$$

where we used $\delta_{\operatorname{succ}(i)} \geq a_{\operatorname{succ}(i)} a_i \beta'^2 4^{-\alpha} > a'_{\operatorname{succ}(i)} a_i \beta'^2 4^{-\alpha}$ (Equation 3.3) for the second step and the identities $a'_{\operatorname{succ}(i)} = 2^{\alpha+1}/\beta'$ and $\ell_i = a_i \delta_i$ for the last one. Finally, observe that the left hand term of this equation is an upper bound on the interference at node i due to the classes $S_j, j \in L^{>\operatorname{succ}(i)}$ such that the desired bound is shown, which completes the proof of Lemma 3.2.12. □

Next we show a bound on the interference induced by the large-loss nodes onto the small-loss nodes.

Lemma 3.2.13. *For every $i \in U$ and $j \in S_i$,*

$$I_{\bar{p}}(j \mid L \setminus \{\operatorname{pred}(i), i\}) \leq \frac{2^{2\alpha+2}}{\beta' \sqrt{\ell_j}} \; .$$

Proof. The proof of this lemma is based on an approach similar to the proof of Lemma 3.2.12. We hence adopt the notation of this proof. The interference

3.2 The Square Root Assignment

when using $\bar{p}$ induced by the nodes from $L^{<\mathrm{pred}(i)}$ on the node $\mathrm{pred}(i)$ can be estimated by

$$\sum_{k \in L^{<\mathrm{pred}(i)}} \frac{\sqrt{\ell_k}}{2^\alpha \delta_{\mathrm{pred}(i)}} \leq \sum_{k \in L^{<\mathrm{pred}(i)}} \frac{\sqrt{\ell_k}}{(d_k + d_{\mathrm{pred}(i)})^\alpha}$$
$$= I_{\bar{p}}(\mathrm{pred}(i) \mid L^{<\mathrm{pred}(i)})$$
$$\leq \frac{2^{\alpha+2}}{\beta' \sqrt{\ell_{\mathrm{pred}(i)}}} .$$

The first bound follows from $(d_k + d_{\mathrm{pred}(i)})^\alpha \leq (2 \cdot d_{\mathrm{pred}(i)})^\alpha = 2^\alpha \delta_{\mathrm{pred}(i)}$. The second bound follows from Lemma 3.2.9 since all nodes in L have a large loss parameter.

Multiplying the above equation with $2^\alpha \delta_{\mathrm{pred}(i)} / \delta_j$

$$I_{\bar{p}}(j \mid L^{<\mathrm{pred}(i)}) \leq \sum_{k \in L^{<\mathrm{pred}(i)}} \frac{\sqrt{\ell_k}}{\delta_j} \leq \frac{2^{2\alpha+2} \cdot \delta_{\mathrm{pred}(i)}}{\beta' \delta_j \sqrt{\ell_{\mathrm{pred}(i)}}}$$
$$= \frac{2^{2\alpha+2} \sqrt{\delta_{\mathrm{pred}(i)}}}{\beta' \delta_j \sqrt{a_{\mathrm{pred}(i)}}} \leq \frac{2^{3\alpha+2}}{\beta'^2 a_{\mathrm{pred}(i)} \sqrt{a_j \delta_j}} \leq \frac{2^{2\alpha+1}}{\beta'^2 \sqrt{\ell_j}} ,$$

where we used $\delta_{\mathrm{pred}(i)} \leq \frac{4^\alpha \delta_j}{\beta'^2 a_j a_{\mathrm{pred}(i)}}$ (Equation 3.3) in the fourth step and $a_{\mathrm{pred}(i)} \geq 2^{\alpha+1}/\beta'$ in the last one.

Using the same kind of arguments, we can bound the interference from nodes in $L^{>i}$ on node i by

$$\sum_{k \in L^{>i}} \frac{\sqrt{\ell_k}}{2^\alpha \delta_k} \leq I_{\bar{p}}(i \mid L^{>i}) \leq \frac{2^{\alpha+2}}{\beta' \sqrt{\ell_i}} .$$

Multiplying with 2^α gives

$$I_{\bar{p}}(j \mid L^{>i}) \leq \sum_{k \in L^{>i}} \frac{\sqrt{\ell_k}}{\delta_k} \leq \frac{2^{2\alpha+2}}{\beta' \sqrt{\ell_i}} \leq \frac{2^{3\alpha+2}}{\beta'^2 a_i \sqrt{\ell_j}} \leq \frac{2^{2\alpha+1}}{\beta' \sqrt{\ell_j}} ,$$

where we used $\ell_i \geq a_i^2 \frac{\beta'^2}{4^\alpha} \ell_j$ (Equation 3.4) and $a_i \geq 2^{\alpha+1}/\beta'$.

Adding the bounds for $I_{\bar{p}}(j \mid L^{<\mathrm{pred}(i)})$ and $I_{\bar{p}}(j \mid L^{>i})$ gives the lemma. □

3. Oblivious Power Assignments and the Bidirectional Model

It remains to show how combining the Lemmas 3.2.9 to 3.2.13 finally lead to Lemma 3.2.4.

The interference at a node $j \in S_i$ for $i \in L$ can be bounded as follows. The interference caused by other nodes with small loss parameter is at most $1/(\beta''\sqrt{\ell_j})$ due to Lemma 3.2.10. The interference caused by nodes $L \setminus \{\text{pred}(i), i\}$ is at most $2^{2\alpha+2}/(\beta'\sqrt{\ell_j})$ due to Lemma 3.2.13. Finally, the interference caused by nodes i and $\text{pred}(i)$ at node j is at most

$$\frac{\sqrt{\ell_{\text{pred}(i)}}}{(d_{\text{pred}(i)} + d_j)^\alpha} + \frac{\sqrt{\ell_i}}{(d_i + d_j)^\alpha} \leq \frac{\sqrt{\ell_{\text{pred}(i)}}}{\beta'\sqrt{\ell_{\text{pred}(i)}\ell_j}} + \frac{\sqrt{\ell_i}}{\beta'\sqrt{\ell_i\ell_j}} = \frac{2}{\beta'\sqrt{\ell_j}} \; .$$

Here, the second step follows because $(d_i+d_j)^{2\alpha} \geq \beta'^2 \ell_i \ell_j$ due to Equation 3.1. In total the interference at j is at most $((2^{2\alpha+2}+2)\frac{1}{\beta'} + \frac{1}{\beta''})\frac{1}{\sqrt{\ell_j}}$. Hence, the nodes with small loss parameters are β-feasible if the constant terms c_0 and c_1 relating β' and β'', respectively, to β satisfy the conditions $c_0 \geq 2^{2\alpha+2} + 2$ and $c_1 \geq 1$.

A slightly more involved argument is required to estimate the interference at a node $i \in L$. The interference due to other nodes in L is at most $2^{\alpha+2}/(\beta'\sqrt{\ell_i})$ by Lemma 3.2.9. The interference caused by nodes in the sets S_j, $j \notin \{i, \text{succ}(i)\}$ is at most $2^\alpha/(\beta''\sqrt{\ell_i})$ by Lemma 3.2.12. The sets S_i and $S_{\text{pred}(i)}$, however, may cause large interference at node i. We use the following trick to deal with this problem: If $|S_i \cup \{i\} \cup S_{\text{succ}(i)}| > \frac{\beta'}{\beta''}$ then we do not choose the node i for the set U in Lemma 3.2.4. We can effort this because only $\mathcal{O}(\frac{\beta''}{\beta'})n = \mathcal{O}(\frac{\beta}{\beta'})n$ satisfy this condition. Now suppose $|S_i \cup \{i\} \cup S_{\text{succ}(i)}| \leq \frac{\beta'}{\beta''}$. Then the interference at i due to these nodes is bounded by

$$\sum_{j \in S_i \cup S_{\text{succ}(i)}} \frac{\sqrt{\ell_j}}{(d_i + d_j)^\alpha} \leq \sum_{j \in S_i \cup S_{\text{succ}(i)}} \frac{\sqrt{\ell_j}}{\beta'\sqrt{\ell_i \ell_j}} \leq \frac{1}{\beta''\sqrt{\ell_i}} \; .$$

Thus, if i is chosen, then the interference at node i is at most $((2^{\alpha+2}+2)\frac{1}{\beta'} + (2^\alpha + 1)\frac{1}{\beta''})\frac{1}{\sqrt{\ell_i}}$. Hence, the nodes with large loss parameters are β-feasible if $c_0 \geq 2^{\alpha+2} + 2$ and $c_1 \geq 2^\alpha + 1$. This completes the proof of Lemma 3.2.4.

3.3 A Scheduling Algorithm for the Square Root Power Assignment

In the *scheduling problem for the square root power assignment*, we are given n bidirectional requests and we seek for a minimal SINR feasible schedule.

Theorem 3.3.1. *There exists a randomized polynomial time approximation algorithm solving the scheduling problem for the square root power assignment with approximation factor $\mathcal{O}(\log n)$.*

Let μ denote the maximal number of requests that can be scheduled in the same step. We will devise an algorithm $\mathcal{A}$ that computes a subset $S \subseteq [n]$ of size $\Omega(\mu)$ with the property that the requests in S can be scheduled in the same step. In order to compute a schedule, algorithm $\mathcal{A}$ is called and the requests in the set S are assigned to the first schedule step. This procedure is repeated recursively on the remaining requests until all requests are scheduled. It is easy to see that such a greedy approach yields an $\mathcal{O}(\log n)$ approximation for an optimal schedule.

We now devise an algorithm $\mathcal{A}$ that has the property described above. In the following, when saying that the SINR constraints are satisfied for a set of requests we mean that they are feasible within a single schedule step. The algorithm partitions the set of communication pairs into disjoint classes. W.l.o.g., let us assume $\min_{j \in [n]} d(u_j, v_j) = 1$ and let k be the smallest integer such that $\max_{j \in [n]} d(u_j, v_j) < 4^{k+1}$. For $0 \leq i \leq k$, class C_i contains the pairs $j \in [n]$ with $4^i \leq d(u_j, v_j) < 4^{i+1}$. This implies that the loss in this class is in $[4^{\alpha i}, 4^{\alpha(i+1)})$. For the time being, let us assume that all requests in class C_i have loss $4^{\alpha i}$ so that the square root power assignment sets the power level to $2^{\alpha i}$. We discuss the consequences of this simplifying assumption at the end of the proof.

The algorithm proceeds as follows. For $i = 0$ to k, it chooses a set S_i of sufficiently many (as defined later) requests from C_i taking into account interference caused by the previously selected sets $S_0, \ldots, S_{i-1}$. In particular, S_i satisfies the SINR constraints with threshold $\beta/2$ *on top of* $S_0, \ldots, S_{i-1}$, i.e., the interference constraints for every pair in S_i are satisfied with threshold $\beta/2$ taking into account the interference caused by the previously inserted pairs in $S_0, \ldots, S_{i-1}$ and the other pairs in S_i. Observe that we relaxed the interference constraints by using the SINR threshold $\beta/2$ instead of β.

3. Oblivious Power Assignments and the Bidirectional Model

Furthermore, choosing S_i might violate the interference constraints of the previously chosen pairs in $S_0, \ldots, S_{i-1}$. We come back to this aspect later.

Let us first take care that the algorithm chooses sufficiently many pairs. Let s_i^* be the maximal size of a subset of requests from C_i such that the SINR constraints at the nodes from S_i are satisfied with original threshold β on top of the pairs in $S_0, \ldots, S_{i-1}$.

Lemma 3.3.2. *There is a polynomial time algorithm choosing S_i such that $|S_i| \geq s_i^*/k_0$, for a suitable constant $k_0 \geq 1$.*

Proof. Let V denote the set of all nodes of the metric. For a node $w \in V$ and a set of requests S, let

$$I(w \mid S) = \sum_{j \in S} \frac{\sqrt{d(u_j, v_j)^\alpha}}{\min\{d(u_j, w)^\alpha, d(v_j, w)^\alpha\}}$$

be the interference at w caused by the pairs in the set S.

Let $S_0 \cup \ldots \cup S_{i-1}$ be fixed. For simplicity of notation, we scale all distances such that the requests in class C_i have distance 1. Let $V' \subseteq V$ denote the subset of nodes with $I(w \mid S_1 \cup \ldots S_{i-1}) < 1/\beta$. Let C_i' denote the subset of requests from C_i only using nodes from V'. S_i^* can take only requests from C_i' as the other pairs exceed the interference threshold. Hence, we only need to take into account nodes from V' and requests from C_i'.

We have to choose a subset $S_i \subseteq C_i'$ of cardinality at least $s_i^*/k_0 = |S_i^*|/k_0$, for a suitable constant k_0. We will choose S_i such that $I(w \mid S_i) < 1/\beta$, for every node w from any pair of S_i. This implies $I(w \mid S_1 \cup \ldots S_{i-1} \cup S_i) < 2/\beta$ as required in the description of the algorithm. The following claim gives a necessary condition that S_i needs to satisfy.

Claim 3.3.3. *Let T be any subset of C_i' satisfying the SINR constraints with threshold β, then for every node in $w \in V'$ it holds $I(w \mid T) < 2^\alpha \beta^{-1}$.*

Proof. If $w = u_k$ or $w = v_k$, for some $k \in T$, then the condition is met directly by the definition of T. Otherwise, let n_k be the node closest to w from (u_k, v_k). Now let $j \in \arg\min_{k \in T} d(n_k, w)$, i.e., n_j is the node from T that is closest to w. By the triangle inequality it holds that $d(n_i, n_j) \leq d(n_i, w) + d(n_j, w) \leq 2d(n_i, w)$ so that $d(n_i, n_j)^\alpha \leq 2^\alpha d(n_i, w)^\alpha$. As a consequence,

$$I(w \mid T) \leq \sum_{i \in T} \frac{1}{d(n_i, w)^\alpha} \leq 2^\alpha \sum_{i \in T} \frac{1}{d(n_i, n_j)^\alpha} < 2^\alpha \beta^{-1}.$$

3.3 A Scheduling Algorithm using Square Root Power

□

The interference constraints from the claim can be described by an ILP with binary variables $x_j \in \{0,1\}$, for $j \in C'_i$, and a linear SINR constraint for every node $w \in V'$. The objective is to maximize $|T| = \sum_{j \in C'_i} x_j$. We relax the integrality requirement and obtain an LP with variables $x_j \in [0,1]$. This LP is solved to optimality. Let x' be the optimal fractional solution and opt' its value. The claim above yields that opt' is an upper bound on s_i^*.

Now we show how to compute a feasible set S_i from x' of cardinality $\Omega(opt')$. We use the randomized rounding technique similar to Proposition 3.2.2. Each request $j \in C_i$ is chosen with probability $x'_j/4 \cdot 2^\alpha$. We assume that the probabilities to be chosen are independent for every pair of distinct requests, that is, the corresponding events are pairwise independent.

Let S' denote the set of chosen requests. This way, for every node $w \in V'$, the expected value of $I(w \mid S')$ is at most $1/4\beta$. Applying the Markov inequality, we observe that w violates the SINR constraint with probability at most $1/4$. Hence, the probability that one of the two nodes of a request from S' violates its SINR constraint is at most $1/2$.

Next we drop those pairs from S' that violate an SINR constraint. S_i is defined to contain the remaining requests. By linearity of expectation, the expected cardinality of S_i is at least $opt'/8 \cdot 2^\alpha$. Hence, the existence of a set S_i of cardinality $opt'/8 \cdot 2^\alpha$ satisfying the SINR constraints is shown.

Analogous to Proposition 3.2.2, this existence proof can be derandomized using the method of pairwise independence, which yields a polynomial time algorithm for computing a set S_i with the properties described in the lemma.

□

The following lemma shows that we have selected $\Omega(\mu)$ requests.

Lemma 3.3.4. $\left| \bigcup_{i=0}^{k} S_i \right| \geq \dfrac{\mu}{k_0 + 2}.$

Proof. In the following let S^* denote a maximum feasible set of requests, that is, $|S^*| = \mu$. Let S_i^* denote the set of those requests in S^* that belong to class C_i. Let $S_{>i} = S_{i+1} \cup \ldots \cup S_k$ and similar indices analogous. Further, for a given subset of pairs S', let $S^*_{\geq i} \mid S'$ denote a maximum subset of $C_{\geq i}$ being feasible on top of S'. We claim

$$\left| S^*_{\geq i+1} \mid S_{<i+1} \right| \geq \left| S^*_{\geq i+1} \mid S_{<i} \right| - 2|S_i| . \qquad (3.7)$$

3. Oblivious Power Assignments and the Bidirectional Model

The claim can be shown by considering the following process. Initially, let $S' = S^*_{\geq i+1} \mid S_{<i}$ and $\bar{S} = S_{<i}$. One after the other, we add the pairs from S_i to $\bar{S}$, each time removing pairs from S' in order to keep the invariant that S' is feasible on top of $\bar{S}$. We will show that it is sufficient to remove at most two pairs from S' for every added pair from S_i. The resulting set S' has thus cardinality at least $|S^*_{\geq i+1} \mid S_{<i}| - 2|S_i|$. It is feasible on top of $S_{<i} \cup S_i = S_{<i+1}$ such that the claim follows.

Consider adding any pair from S_i to $\bar{S}$. We add the two nodes of this pair one after the other and show that the addition of each of them can be compensated by removing at most one pair from S'. Let u be any of the two nodes from the considered pair. Let v be the node from a pair in S' that is closest to u. Then, for every $w \in S'$, it holds $d(v,w) \leq d(v,u) + d(u,w) \leq 2d(u,w)$ so that $d(v,w)^\alpha \leq 2^\alpha d(u,w)^\alpha$. As a consequence,

$$I_{\bar{p}}(w \mid v) \geq \frac{\sqrt{4^{\alpha(i+1)}}}{d(v,w)^\alpha} \geq \frac{\sqrt{4^{\alpha(i+1)}}}{2^\alpha d(u,w)^\alpha} = \frac{\sqrt{4^{\alpha i}}}{d(u,w)^\alpha} = I_{\bar{p}}(w \mid u) \ .$$

(W.l.o.g., we assumed $d(v,w)^\alpha > 0$ and, hence, $d(u,w)^\alpha > 0$. Observe that $d(v,w)^\alpha = 0$ would imply that S' is not feasible on top of $\bar{S}$, which contradicts our invariant.) Hence, when adding u and removing v the interference at any node w from S' does not increase. Consequently, the addition of a pair can be compensated by removing at most two pairs, one for each node of the pair. This proves Equation 3.7.

With the help of this equation, we will now prove the following claim. For $0 \leq i \leq k$, it holds

$$|S_{\geq i}| \geq \frac{1}{k_0 + 2} \left| S^*_{\geq i} \mid S_{<i} \right| \ . \tag{3.8}$$

Observe that this claim yields the lemma when setting $i = 0$.

The claim is shown by a downward induction. For $i = k$ its correctness follows from Lemma 3.3.2. Now assume the claim holds for $i + 1$. Then

$$|S_{\geq i}| = |S_i| + |S_{\geq i+1}| \geq |S_i| + \frac{1}{k_0 + 2} \left| S^*_{\geq i+1} \mid S_{<i+1} \right| \ .$$

Applying Equation 3.7 gives

$$|S_{\geq i}| \geq |S_i| + \frac{1}{k_0 + 2} \left(\left| S^*_{\geq i+1} \mid S_{<i} \right| - 2|S_i| \right)$$

3.3 A Scheduling Algorithm using Square Root Power

$$= \frac{1}{k_0+2} \left(|S^*_{\geq i+1}| \, |S_{<i}| + k_0 \, |S_i| \right) .$$

Finally, applying Lemma 3.3.2 gives

$$|S_{\geq i}| \geq \frac{1}{k_0+2} \left(|S^*_i| \, |S_{<i}| + |S^*_{\geq i+1}| \, |S_{<i}| \right) \geq \frac{1}{k_0+2} |S^*_{\geq i}| \, |S_{<i}|$$

Thus Equation 3.8 is shown, which completes the proof of Lemma 3.3.4. □

Notice, when the algorithm computes S_i, it ensures that the interference constraints for S_i on top of $S_0, \ldots, S_{i-1}$ are satisfied with SINR threshold $\beta/2$. The algorithm does not explicitly take care for the additional interference caused by adding the pairs in S_i at the pairs from $S_0, \ldots, S_{i-1}$. The following lemma, however, shows that this increase is bounded by a constant factor.

Lemma 3.3.5. *There is constant $k_1 \geq 1$ such that $\bigcup_{i=0}^{k} S_i$ satisfies the SINR constraints with threshold at most β/k_1.*

Proof. Let us first make the following useful observation: The distance between a node u of a pair from set S_i and a node v of a pair from set S_j, $j \geq i$, is at least $2^{(i+j)-1/\alpha} \beta$ as, otherwise, the strength the signals received by v from u would be larger than the interference threshold $(2^{\alpha j-1} \beta)^{-1}$ that the algorithm enforces for the pairs in S_j.

W.l.o.g., let us consider a node u_0 of a request from the set S_0. The proof for other classes is analogous. We need to show that the sum of the signals due to the requests in $S_1 \cup \ldots S_k$ received by u_0 is at most $k_1 \beta^{-1}$.

Fix $i \in \{1, \ldots, k\}$. Let $(u_1, v_1), \ldots, (u_t, v_t)$ denote the requests in S_i. For the ease of notation, let u_j be the node located closer to u_0, for each pair (u_j, v_j). Let, furthermore, $d(u_1, u_0)^\alpha \leq d(u_2, u_0)^\alpha \leq \cdots \leq d(u_t, u_0)^\alpha$. From the triangle inequality we can conclude $d(u_j, u_1) \leq d(u_j, u_0) + d(u_0, u_1) \leq 2d(u_j, u_0)$ so that $d(u_j, u_1)^\alpha \leq 2^\alpha d(u_j, u_0)^\alpha$. Hence, the sum of the signals received by u_0 from the pairs in $S_i \setminus \{(u_1, v_1)\}$ can be bounded from above by

$$\sum_{j=2}^{t} \frac{\sqrt{4^{\alpha i}}}{d(u_j, u_0)^\alpha} \leq 2^\alpha \sum_{j=2}^{t} \frac{\sqrt{4^{\alpha i}}}{d(u_j, u_1)^\alpha} < \frac{2^{\alpha+1}}{2^{-\alpha i} \beta} \leq \frac{4}{2^{-i} \beta} .$$

Here the second inequality follows from the fact that the interference threshold at u_1 is $2^{-\alpha i+1}/\beta$. Summing the above bound over all sets $S_1, \ldots, S_k$ gives an upper bound of $\mathcal{O}(\beta^{-1})$ on the interference caused by those pairs not being the closest pair to u_0 in their class.

65

3. Oblivious Power Assignments and the Bidirectional Model

It remains to take care for the interference caused by those pairs from each class that are closest to u_0. Let $(u_1, v_1) \in S_1, \ldots, (u_k, v_k) \in S_k$ denote pairs such that u_i is the closest node to u_0 over all nodes from pairs in S_i. We need to show that the sum of signals received from these nodes at u_0 is bounded by $\mathcal{O}(\beta^{-1})$ as well. Let

$$i(1) = \arg\min_{i \in \{1,\ldots,k\}} d(u_0, u_i)^\alpha,$$
$$i(2) = \arg\min_{i \in \{i(1),\ldots,k\}} d(u_0, u_i)^\alpha,$$
$$i(3) = \arg\min_{i \in \{i(2),\ldots,k\}} d(u_0, u_i)^\alpha,$$

and so on until one reaches an index $i(q)$ with $i(q) = k$. To extend our notation, let $i(0) = 0$.

By our observation from above, for $1 \leq r \leq q$, it holds $d(u_{i(r-1)}, u_{i(r)}) \geq 2^{(i(r)+i(r-1))-1/\alpha}\beta$. Let $\gamma = 2^{-1-1/\alpha}\beta^{1/\alpha}$. Then

$$d(u_{i(r-1)}, u_{i(r)}) \geq \gamma 2^{i(r)+i(r-1)+1} \geq \gamma 2^{i(r)+r}$$

since $i(r-1) \geq r-1$. From this lower bound for $d(u_{i(r-1)}, u_{i(r)})$, we derive now a lower bound for $d(u_{i(r)}, u_0)$. For the purpose of a contradiction, assume $d(u_{i(r)}, u_0) < \gamma 2^{i(r)+r-1}$, for some $1 \leq r \leq q$. Then, as the distance from $u_{i(r-1)}$ to u_0 is not larger than the distance from $u_{i(r)}$, it follows $d(u_{i(r-1)}, u_0) < \gamma 2^{i(r)+r-1}$, too. As a consequence,

$$d(u_{i(r)}, u_0) \geq d(u_{i(r)}, u_{i(r-1)}) - d(u_{i(r-1)}, u_0)$$
$$\geq \gamma 2^{i(r)+r} - \gamma 2^{i(r)+r-1} \geq \gamma 2^{i(r)+r-1}.$$

This way, the strength of the signals received at u_0 can be bounded from above by

$$\sum_{r=1}^{q} \sum_{j=i(r-1)+1}^{i(r)} \frac{2^{\alpha j}}{d(u_{i(r)}, u_0)^\alpha} \leq \sum_{r=1}^{q} \sum_{j=i(r-1)+1}^{i(r)} \frac{2^{\alpha j}}{2^{\alpha(i(r)+r-1)}} \gamma^{-\alpha}$$
$$\leq \sum_{r=1}^{q} \frac{2^{\alpha i(r)+1}}{2^{\alpha(i(r)+r-1)}} \gamma^{-\alpha}$$
$$= \mathcal{O}(\gamma^{-\alpha})$$

3.3 A Scheduling Algorithm using Square Root Power

$$= \mathcal{O}(\beta^{-1}) ,$$

which completes the proof of Lemma 3.3.5. □

Lemma 3.3.2 and 3.3.4 show that the algorithm chooses $\Omega(\mu)$ requests. However, these requests might violate the SINR constraints with threshold β because of the following reasons: a) We assumed that the loss in class C_i is exactly $4^{-\alpha i}$ rather than from the interval $[4^{\alpha i}, 4^{\alpha(i+1)})$. b) The pairs in each set S_i are chosen with respect to a relaxed SINR threshold $\beta/2$ instead of β. c) The SINR constraints for the sets in $S_0, \ldots, S_{i-1}$ are not explicitly considered when choosing S_i. (a) and (b) obviously increase the interference at most by a constant factor. Lemma 3.3.5 shows that the same is true for (c). Hence, the SINR constraints are violated at most by a constant factor so that they can be thinned out by applying Proposition 3.2.2. This way, one obtains a feasible set S of cardinality $\Omega(\mu)$. Thus, Theorem 3.3.1 is shown.

3. Oblivious Power Assignments and the Bidirectional Model

Chapter 4
Online Request Scheduling

In this chapter we study the online variant of the capacity maximization problem. We consider sets of directed and bidirectional requests, as well as mixed sets of requests. For notational simplicity, we will treat bidirectional requests as two directed requests using the same power in the right-hand side of the SINR constraint (Equation 1.1). For most of this chapter, we assume requests lie in $\mathbb{R}^d$ of constant dimension d, and the distance function is an l_p-norm or the l_{max}-norm. In this chapter we consider Euclidean *fading metrics* [Hal09], i.e., we require that $\alpha > d$, where we treat both α and d as constants. For simplicity we assume that noise is absent, $N_1 = \ldots = N_k = 0$. Our algorithms will satisfy the SINR constraint with strict inequality. This allows to scale powers up sufficiently to satisfy the constraints also when there is noise. Clearly, such a scaling might be wasteful or infeasible in practice, but this aspect is beyond our analysis. When there is no noise, we can scale all distances such that $\min_i d(u_i, v_i) = 1$ and $\max_i d(u_i, v_i) = \Delta$.

To the best of our knowledge there are no theoretical results for this problem in an online scenario. Thus, we seek to analyze bounds for uniform and linear as well as for square root power assignments. We generalize these three classes to *polynomial* assignments of the form $\phi(d(u_i, v_i)) = d(u_i, v_i)^{r\alpha}$ with parameter $r \in \mathbb{R}$. For uniqueness we assume ϕ is always scaled such that $\phi(1) = 1$.

We first analyze only the spatial aspect of the problem on a single channel and give algorithm SAFE-DISTANCE and a general lower bound. In Section 4.2 we give the near-optimal algorithm MULTI-CLASS SAFE-DISTANCE (Section 4.2.1), the generalization to k channels (Section 4.2.2) and the randomized algorithm (Section 4.2.3). In Section 4.3 we reach the full level

4. Online Request Scheduling

of generality by describing the adjustments to requests with duration (Section 4.3.1) and to doubling metrics (Section 4.3.2).

4.1 A Simple Algorithm and a Lower Bound

In the following we first analyze the spatial aspect of the problem and assume that requests last forever, i.e., for all requests i, $t_i = \infty$. We begin by analyzing a simple online algorithm for the case of a single channel and any polynomial power assignment. Subsequently, we show a general lower bound. Our analysis of the online algorithm introduces a number of critical observations that we use in later sections.

The main idea of the algorithm is to accept a new request only if it keeps a *safe distance* σ from every other previously accepted request. In particular, we accept incoming request i only if $\min\{d(u_i, v_j), d(u_j, v_i)\} \geq \sigma$ for every other previously accepted request $j \in S$. We call this algorithm SAFE-DISTANCE.

Algorithm 4 SAFE-DISTANCE

1: Initialize accepted requests $S = \emptyset$.
2: **while** a new request i arrives **do**
3:    Set $p_i = \phi(d(u_i, v_i))$ and temporarily accept $S' \leftarrow S \cup i$
4:    **for all** $j \in S$ **do**
5:       **if** $\min\{d(u_i, v_j), d(u_j, v_i)\} \leq \sigma$ **then**
6:          decline request: $S' \leftarrow S$.
7:       **end if**
8:    **end for**
9:    Update: $S \leftarrow S'$.
10: **end while**

For the choice of σ there is a conflict between correctness and competitive ratio. A larger σ blocks out a larger portion of the space, in which an optimal algorithm knowing the request sequence might be able to accept requests. If σ is too small, then at some point the interference at an accepted request can get too large and the SINR constraint becomes violated.

We strive to choose σ as small as possible to ensure correctness of SAFE-DISTANCE. To bound the interference at accepted requests we construct a worst-case scenario. We consider a receiver v_i from a single accepted request

4.1 A Simple Algorithm and a Lower Bound

and bound the maximum number of senders that can be at a certain distance from v_i. In the following we show that for $r \in [0,1]$ the choice of

$$\sigma = \max\left\{2\Delta, \Delta \cdot 18d \cdot \sqrt[\alpha]{\frac{2\beta}{(\alpha-d)}}\right\}$$

is sufficient to yield the following result.

Theorem 4.1.1. SAFE-DISTANCE *is* $\mathcal{O}(\Delta^d)$-*competitive for any polynomial power assignment with* $r \in [0,1]$ *and a single channel.*

Proof. We first show that SAFE-DISTANCE is correct, i.e., for an accepted request i the SINR constraint of i never becomes violated. In particular, we will underestimate the distances of accepted senders of other requests to overestimate the interference at receiver v_i. However, even under such pessimistic conditions the SINR constraint at v_i will remain valid.

Consider a receiver v_i of an accepted request i. To estimate the interference at v_i we have to count how many senders may be placed at which distance. Using $\sigma \geq 2\Delta$ and the choice rule of the algorithm it is straightforward to verify that senders of any two different accepted requests are at least a distance of $\sigma - \Delta \geq \sigma/2$ apart. We segment all of $\mathbb{R}^d$ into d-dimensional hypercubes with length $\sigma/3d$, which we call *sectors*. The greatest distance within a sector is $\sigma d/3d = \sigma/3 < \sigma/2$. Each sector can contain senders from at most one request, so there are at most 2 senders in every sector (in the case of a bidirectional request). Without loss of generality, we assume that sectors are created such that v_i lies in a corner point of 2^d sectors. We divide the set of sectors into *layers*. The first layer are the 2^d sectors incident to v_i. The second layer are all sectors that are not in the first layer but share at least a point with a sector from the first layer, and so on. Figure 4.1 shows an example of this segmentation for the Euclidean plane.

In this construction there are exactly $(2\ell)^d$ sectors from layers 1 through ℓ, and their union is a hypercube of side length $2\ell\sigma/3d$ with v_i in the center. Therefore, there are exactly $2^d(\ell^d - (\ell-1)^d)$ sectors in layer ℓ.

Due to the algorithm there can be no sender at a distance smaller than σ from v_i. The sector of smallest layer that is at a distance at least σ from r_i can be reached along the volume diagonal of the layer hypercubes. There can be no sender in all sectors from layers 1 through ℓ', where ℓ' is bounded by $\sigma \leq \ell'(\sigma/3)$, which yields $\ell' \geq 3$. For bounding the interference assume

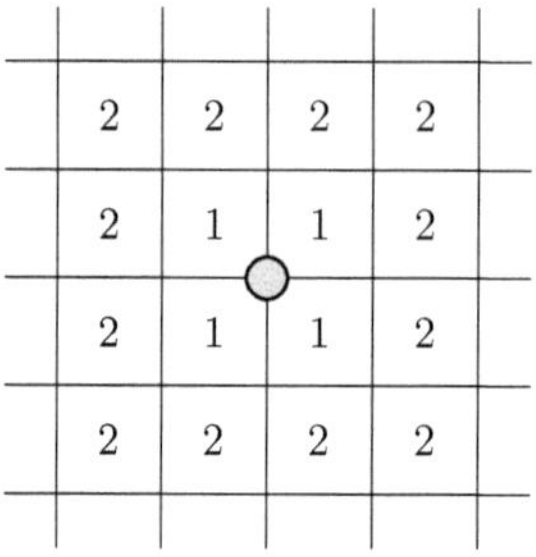

4. Online Request Scheduling

2	2	2	2
2	1	1	2
2	1	1	2
2	2	2	2

Figure 4.1: Distribution of sectors of the first two layers around a receiver in the Euclidean plane.

that in all sectors of layer $\ell \geq 3$ there are 2 senders. Note that all senders in sectors from a layer ℓ have a distance at least $(\ell-1)\sigma/3d$ to v_i. To bound the interference that is created at v_i, we use the following technical lemma.

Lemma 4.1.2. *For $\alpha > d \geq 1$ it holds that*

$$2^d \cdot \sum_{l=3}^{\infty} \frac{\ell^d - (\ell-1)^d}{(\ell-1)^\alpha} < \frac{6^d}{\alpha - d}.$$

Proof. We observe

$$2^d \cdot \sum_{\ell=3}^{\infty} \frac{\ell^d - (\ell-1)^d}{(\ell-1)^\alpha}$$
$$\leq 2^d \cdot \sum_{\ell=3}^{\infty} \frac{2^d \ell^{d-1}}{(\ell-1)^\alpha}$$
$$= 2^{2d} \cdot \sum_{\ell=3}^{\infty} \frac{\ell^{d-1}}{(\ell-1)^\alpha}.$$

We now bound $l^{d-1}/(l-1)^\alpha$, where we assume that $\epsilon = \alpha - d > 0$. This

4.1 A Simple Algorithm and a Lower Bound

yields

$$2^{2d} \cdot \sum_{\ell=3}^{\infty} \frac{\ell^{d-1}}{(\ell-1)^\alpha}$$

$$= 2^{2d} \cdot \sum_{\ell=3}^{\infty} \frac{\ell^{d-1}}{(\ell-1)^{d-1}} \cdot \frac{1}{(\ell-1)^{1+\epsilon}}$$

$$= 2^{2d} \cdot \sum_{\ell=3}^{\infty} \left(1 + \frac{1}{\ell-1}\right)^{d-1} \cdot \frac{1}{(\ell-1)^{1+\epsilon}}$$

$$< 6^d \cdot \sum_{\ell=3}^{\infty} \frac{1}{(\ell-1)^{1+\epsilon}}$$

$$= 6^d \cdot \sum_{\ell=2}^{\infty} \ell^{-1-\epsilon} .$$

The assumption $\epsilon > 0$ yields a constant value for the expression, which is $6^d \cdot (\zeta(1+\epsilon) - 1)$. We estimate this value by $\sum_{\ell=2}^{\infty} \ell^{-1-\epsilon} < \int_{\ell=1}^{\infty} \ell^{-1-\epsilon} = 1/\epsilon$, which proves the lemma. $\square$

This yields

$$I = \sum_{j \in S, j \neq i} \frac{d(u_i, v_i)^{r\alpha}}{d(u_j, v_i)^\alpha}$$

$$\leq 2\Delta^{r\alpha} \sum_{\ell=3}^{\infty} 2^d (\ell^d - (\ell-1)^d) \cdot \frac{1}{((\ell-1)\sigma/3d)^\alpha}$$

$$< 2\Delta^{r\alpha} \left(\frac{3d}{\sigma}\right)^\alpha \cdot \frac{6^d}{\alpha - d} .$$

Note that the SINR constraint is satisfied if $p_i/d(u_i, v_i)^\alpha \geq \Delta^{r\alpha}/\Delta^\alpha \geq \beta I$, or

$$2\beta\Delta^{r\alpha} \cdot \left(\frac{3d}{\sigma}\right)^\alpha \cdot \frac{6^d}{\alpha - d} \leq \Delta^{(r-1)\alpha} .$$

This yields a lower bound for the distance of

$$\sigma \geq \Delta \cdot 3d \cdot \sqrt[\alpha]{\frac{2\beta 6^d}{\alpha - d}} , \qquad (4.1)$$

which can be verified to hold for our choice of σ.

4. Online Request Scheduling

To bound the competitive ratio we need the following *Density Lemma*, which is an extension of Lemma 3 in [AD09] to both senders and receivers, and to metric spaces of arbitrary dimension d. The proof requires some adjustments from [AD09].

Lemma 4.1.3 (Density Lemma). *Consider a sector A with side-length $x \geq 1$ and any feasible solution with arbitrary power assignment. There can be only $(d+1)^\alpha x^d/\beta$ requests with a receiver in A and only $(d+1)^\alpha x^d/\beta$ requests with a sender in A.*

Proof. We first assume $x = 1$ and consider the number of receivers and senders in A separately.

Receivers: We first prove the lemma for the receivers. Let us assume that the transmission powers in the solution are such that there is a constant $\bar{p}$ such that the signal strength received by a receiver $p_i/d(u_i, v_i)^\alpha = \bar{p}$ for any request with $v_i \in A$. Consider another request with $v_j \in A$. The interference of j at v_i is $p_j/d(u_j, v_i)^\alpha \geq p_j/(d(v_i, v_j) + d(u_j, v_j))^\alpha$. Due to the size of the sector we have that $d(v_i, v_j) \leq d$. Also $d(u_j, v_j) \geq 1$, which implies

$$\frac{p_j}{(d(v_i, v_j) + d(u_j, v_j))^\alpha} \geq \frac{1}{(d+1)^\alpha} \cdot \frac{p_j}{d(u_j, v_j)^\alpha} \geq \frac{\bar{p}}{(d+1)^\alpha}.$$

Thus, if more than $(d+1)^\alpha/\beta$ such connections are present, the SINR constraint *for all of them* is violated.

Now consider a solution with arbitrary powers. Here we artificially reduce powers such that all connections experience a minimal signal strength $\bar{p}$ and then increase powers to their original value. The increase deteriorates SINR ratios for the requests that continue to have a signal strength of $\bar{p}$. Hence, if more than $(d+1)^\alpha/\beta$ receivers are present in A, *at least one* SINR constraint is violated.

Senders: For bounding the number of senders in A we use a similar approach. This time, however, we first assume that all senders use the same transmission power. Thus, for two requests i and j this yields $p_j/d(u_j, v_i)^\alpha \geq p_j/(d(u_i, u_j) + d(u_i, v_i))^\alpha$. We have that $d(u_i, u_j) \leq d$. Also $d(u_j, v_j) \geq 1$, so $p_j/(d(u_j, u_i) + d(u_i, v_i))^\alpha \geq \frac{1}{(d+1)^\alpha} \cdot \frac{p_j}{d(u_i, v_i)^\alpha}$ as

4.1 A Simple Algorithm and a Lower Bound

before. Thus, for the SINR constraint it is necessary that

$$\frac{p_i}{d(u_i, v_i)^\alpha} \geq \frac{\beta}{(d+1)^\alpha} \cdot \sum_{j \neq i} \frac{p_j}{d(u_i, v_i)^\alpha}.$$

Using $p_i = p_j$ for all requests i and j, there can be at most $(d+1)^\alpha/\beta$ senders in A, otherwise the SINR constraint *for all* requests is violated. A similar observation as before generalizes the argument to arbitrary powers.

This proves the lemma for $x = 1$. If $x > 1$ we can divide A into sectors of length 1, apply the above arguments, and the bound follows. □

The density lemma allows a simple way to bound the number of connections the optimum solution can accept in the blocked area. First consider a sender u_i of a request accepted by SAFE-DISTANCE. The sender blocks a hypersphere of radius σ for receivers of other requests. We overestimate its size by a sector of side-length 2σ centered at u_i. By the density lemma, the optimum solution can accept at most $(d+1)^\alpha (2\sigma)^d/\beta$ requests, which is $\mathcal{O}(\Delta^d)$ for fixed α, β, and d. For the receiver v_i there is a similar estimation. This time we bound the number of senders in a hypersphere around v_i, which is $\mathcal{O}(\Delta^d)$ for fixed α, β, and d. Finally, note that σ is chosen to maximize conceptual simplicity and does not optimize the involved constants in the competitive ratio. □

We can use similar arguments to show a result for any other polynomial power assignment. As safe distance we pick $\sigma^+ = \Delta^r \cdot \sigma$ if $r > 1$, and $\sigma^- = \Delta^{1-r} \cdot \sigma$ if $r < 0$.

Corollary 4.1.4. *Algorithm* SAFE-DISTANCE *is* $\mathcal{O}\left(\Delta^{d \cdot \max\{r, 1-r\}}\right)$*-competitive for a polynomial power assignment with* $r \notin (0,1)$ *and a single channel.*

Proof. In the case $r > 1$ we note for correctness of the algorithm that the interference at an accepted receiver v_i is again bounded by

$$\begin{aligned} I &= \sum_{j \in S, j \neq i} d(u_j, v_j)^{r\alpha}/d(u_j, v_i)^\alpha \\ &\leq \Delta^{r\alpha} \sum_{j \in S, j \neq i} 1/d(u_j, v_i)^\alpha \end{aligned}$$

4. Online Request Scheduling

$$< 2\Delta^{r\alpha} \cdot \left(\frac{3d}{\sigma^+}\right)^\alpha \cdot \frac{6^d}{\alpha - d} .$$

The SINR constraint now requires that $p_i/d(u_i, v_i)^\alpha = d(u_i, v_i)^{(r-1)\alpha} \geq 1 \geq \beta I$. This yields a lower bound of

$$\sigma^+ \geq \Delta^r \cdot 3d \cdot \sqrt[\alpha]{\frac{2\beta 6^d}{\alpha - d}} . \tag{4.2}$$

Bounding the competitive ratio can be done as before and proves the result for the case $r > 1$.

If $r < 0$, then the interference is maximized with requests of length 1 in each sector. The interference is thus bounded by

$$I = \sum_{j \in S, j \neq i} d(u_j, v_j)^{r\alpha}/d(u_j, v_i)^\alpha \leq \sum_{j \in S, j \neq i} 1/d(u_j, v_i)^\alpha < 2 \cdot \left(\frac{3d}{\sigma^-}\right)^\alpha \cdot \frac{6^d}{\alpha - d} .$$

The SINR constraint now requires that

$$p_i/d(u_i, v_i)^\alpha = d(u_i, v_i)^{(r-1)\alpha} \geq \Delta^{(r-1)\alpha} \geq \beta I .$$

This yields a lower bound

$$\sigma^- \geq \Delta^{1-r} \cdot 3d \cdot \sqrt[\alpha]{\frac{2\beta 6^d}{\alpha - d}} . \tag{4.3}$$

The corollary follows. □

As it turns out, the competitive ratio of SAFE-DISTANCE is asymptotically best possible for polynomial power assignments with $r \notin (0, 1)$. This includes both the uniform and linear power assignment. Next, we bound the competitive ratio for any deterministic online algorithm using polynomial power assignments. This can be generalized to a lower bound for any distance-based power assignment.

Theorem 4.1.5. *Every deterministic online algorithm using a polynomial power assignment has a competitive ratio of $\Omega\left(\Delta^{d \cdot \max\{r, 1-r\}}\right)$. Every deterministic online algorithm is $\Omega\left(\Delta^{d/2}\right)$-competitive*

- *using arbitrary power assignments in the case of bidirectional requests and*

4.1 A Simple Algorithm and a Lower Bound

- using distance-based power assignments in the case of only directed requests.

Proof. The main observation in the proof is that every deterministic online algorithm has to accept the first request that arrives, otherwise it risks having an unbounded competitive ratio. While this is true only for strictly competitive algorithms, we can repeat the following instance sufficiently often and keep a sufficiently large distance between the instances. In this way we can neglect the constant a from the competitive ratio.

We first consider the case that all requests are directed and polynomial power assignment. Let the first request have length Δ. From the SINR constraint we bound the minimum distance every other successful request has to keep to sender u_1 or receiver v_1. This yields a blocked area in which the online algorithm is not able to accept any request. We then count the maximum number of requests that can be placed into this area, and which the optimum solution can accept simultaneously. The next Proposition yields a bound on the minimum distance between two requests with a polynomial power assignment.

Proposition 4.1.6. *Consider two directed successful requests i and j with polynomial power assignment. The distance between s_i and r_j must be at least $d(u_i, v_j) \geq \sqrt[\alpha]{\beta} \cdot d(u_i, v_i)^r \cdot d(u_j, v_j)^{1-r}$.*

Proof. Consider the SINR constraint for request j when only requests i and j are accepted. It reads

$$d(u_j, v_j)^{\alpha(r-1)} \geq \beta(d(u_i, v_i)^{r\alpha}/d(u_i, v_j)^{\alpha}) ,$$

and rearranging yields the result. □

Now suppose the online algorithm has accepted the first request of length Δ. The adversary subsequently presents requests of length 1. If the sender of one such request is closer than $\sqrt[\alpha]{\beta} \cdot \Delta^{1-r}$ to v_1, the online algorithm cannot accept the request. The same holds if the receiver is closer than $\sqrt[\alpha]{\beta} \cdot \Delta^r$ to u_1. Thus, there are two hyperspherical areas blocked around sender and receiver of request 1. Let us consider the case $r \leq 0.5$ and the hypersphere around the receiver. All subsequent arguments follow similarly for $r > 0.5$ and the sender.

77

4. Online Request Scheduling

The adversary can place requests, all of equal length $d(u_i, v_i) = 1$, into the hypersphere of radius $\sqrt[\alpha]{\beta} \cdot \Delta^r$ around v_1. Similar to the proof of Theorem 4.1.1 we divide the space into sectors of length $2\sigma_1$, where

$$\sigma_1 = \max\left\{2, 18d \cdot \sqrt[\alpha]{\frac{2\beta}{(\alpha - d)}}\right\}.$$

We again assume that v_1 is located on the boundary of d sectors. How many sectors are completely enclosed by the blocked hypersphere around v_1? The side-length of the maximum hypercube that is contained is $2\Delta \sqrt[\alpha]{\beta}/d$. There are at least $\frac{2\Delta \sqrt[\alpha]{\beta}}{d\sigma_1} - 1$ sectors along each dimension within the hypercube, a number in $\Theta(\Delta^r)$. This obviously yields a total number of $\Omega(\Delta^{rd})$ sectors, in which the online algorithm must not accept any request. However, we observe that σ_1 is chosen using the formula for σ with ratio 1. It is possible to locate one request of length 1 in each sector such that receivers and senders of two different requests are at least a distance of σ_1 apart. By Theorem 4.1.1 it is possible to accept all these $\Omega(\Delta^{rd})$ small requests simultaneously, which proves the theorem for case $r \leq 0.5$. For $r > 0.5$ we can place requests in the hypersphere around s_1 to derive a similar result.

To extend the previous arguments to arbitrary distance-based power assignments, we observe that the previous lower bound uses only requests of length 1 and Δ. Let ϕ be the function of the distance-based power assignment, then $\phi(\Delta)$ is the power of the first request. The lower bound for this power assignment behaves exactly as for a polynomial assignment with $r = (\log \phi(\Delta))/(\alpha \log \Delta)$.

Note that when a power assignment is not distance-based, it might assign different powers to small requests based on whether they are near the sender or the receiver of the first request. This, however, does not help if the requests are bidirectional. In this case we create the same instance using only bidirectional requests. Then we get a blocked area of at least $\Omega\left(\Delta^{d/2}\right)$ for any polynomial power assignment around both points of the first request. Using the normalization of powers as before we observe that there is a blocked area of size $\Omega\left(\Delta^{d/2}\right)$ for any small request, *no matter which power we assign to it*. This proves the theorem. □

4.2 Competitive Ratios below Δ^d

4.2.1 A Near-Optimal Algorithm for the Square Root Assignment

In this section we extend algorithm SAFE-DISTANCE to achieve a competitive ratio, which is close to the best-possible ratio for any distance-based power assignment. The algorithm uses the square root power assignment, and the main idea of the algorithm is to block areas based on the distances of the involved requests. In particular, we classify requests into m length classes, where class $\mathcal{C}_x$ contains requests i with $d(u_i, v_i) \in [\Delta^{a_x}, \Delta^{a_{x-1}}]$ with $a_x = 1/2^x$, for $x = 1, \ldots, m-1$ and $[1, \Delta^{a_{m-1}}]$ for class $\mathcal{C}_m$. With each class we associate a safe distance $\sigma(\mathcal{C}_x)$ chosen as

$$\sigma(\mathcal{C}_x) = \max\left\{2\Delta^{a_{x-1}}, \Delta^{0.5+a_x} \cdot 18d \cdot \sqrt[\alpha]{2\beta m \cdot \left(2 + \frac{1}{\alpha - d}\right)}\right\}.$$

Algorithm 5 MULTI-CLASS SAFE-DISTANCE
1: Initialize accepted requests $S = \emptyset$.
2: **while** a new request i arrives **do**
3:     Set $p_i = \sqrt{d(u_i, v_i)^\alpha}$ and temporarily accept $S' \leftarrow S \cup i$
4:     **for all** $j \in S$ **do**
5:       Let $\mathcal{C}_x$ and $\mathcal{C}_y$ be the length classes of requests i and j, respectively
6:       **if** $\min\{d(u_i, v_j), d(u_j, v_i)\} \leq \min\{\sigma(\mathcal{C}_x), \sigma(\mathcal{C}_y)\}$ **then**
7:         decline request: $S' \leftarrow S$.
8:     **end if**
9:     **end for**
10:    Update: $S \leftarrow S'$.
11: **end while**

This yields the following result.

Theorem 4.2.1. *For any constant $\varepsilon > 0$, MULTI-CLASS SAFE-DISTANCE is $\mathcal{O}\left(\Delta^{d/2+\varepsilon}\right)$-competitive for a single channel.*

Proof. We first show that the algorithm is correct. We again treat a single accepted request and bound the interference from other accepted requests. This time, however, we have to consider the class the request is contained

4. Online Request Scheduling

in. Suppose a request i is from class $\mathcal{C}_x$. To show that it is successful we have to estimate the distances $d(u_j, v_i)$ for other requests. We will bound the interference from requests of each class separately and apply the construction outlined in Theorem 4.1.1. For requests of class $\mathcal{C}_y$ we assume a worst-case placement and divide the space into sectors of side-length $\sigma(\mathcal{C}_y)/3d$. This again shows that no sector can contain more than two senders. The consideration of layers allows to bound the joint interference from all senders. For a class $y \geq x$, the minimum distance from v_i to each sender is at least $\sigma(\mathcal{C}_y)$. Thus, there is no sender in layers 1 and 2, and we can apply previous arguments to bound the interference. For classes with $y < x$ we note that the minimum distance between v_i and any sender from this class is only $\sigma(\mathcal{C}_x) < \sigma(\mathcal{C}_y)$. Senders can be closer to v_i creating more interference. In particular, we lose the property that there are no senders in sectors of layers 1 and 2. Instead, for these senders we explicitly bound the distance using $\sigma(\mathcal{C}_x)$.

$$
\begin{aligned}
I &\leq \sum_{y=1}^{m} \sum_{j \in \mathcal{C}_y, j \neq i} \frac{d(u_j, v_j)^{\alpha/2}}{d(u_j, v_i)^\alpha} \leq \sum_{y \geq x} \sum_{j \in \mathcal{C}_y, j \neq i} \frac{\Delta^{\alpha/2^y}}{d(u_j, v_i)^\alpha} + \sum_{y < x} \sum_{j \in \mathcal{C}_y} \frac{\Delta^{\alpha/2^y}}{d(u_j, v_i)^\alpha} \\
&< \sum_{y \geq x} 2\Delta^{\alpha/2^y} \cdot \left(\frac{3d}{\sigma(\mathcal{C}_y)}\right)^\alpha \cdot \frac{6^d}{\alpha - d} + \underbrace{\sum_{y < x} \Delta^{\alpha/2^y} \sum_{j \in \mathcal{C}_y} \frac{1}{d(u_j, v_i)^\alpha}}_{I^{<x}}
\end{aligned}
$$

With Lemma 4.1.2 we observe

$$
\begin{aligned}
I^{<x} &\leq 2 \sum_{y<x} \Delta^{\alpha/2^y} \cdot \left(\frac{2^d}{\sigma(\mathcal{C}_x)^\alpha} + \left(\frac{3d}{\sigma(\mathcal{C}_y)}\right)^\alpha \cdot \left(4^d + 2^d \sum_{\ell=3}^{\infty} \frac{\ell^d - (\ell-1)^d}{(\ell-1)^\alpha}\right)\right) \\
&< \sum_{y<x} 2\Delta^{\alpha/2^y} \cdot \left(\frac{2^d}{\sigma(\mathcal{C}_x)^\alpha} + \left(\frac{3d}{\sigma(\mathcal{C}_y)}\right)^\alpha \cdot \left(4^d + \frac{6^d}{\alpha - d}\right)\right) \\
&\leq \sum_{y<x} 2\Delta^{\alpha/2^y} \cdot \left(\frac{3d}{\sigma(\mathcal{C}_x)}\right)^\alpha \cdot 6^d \cdot \left(2 + \frac{1}{\alpha - d}\right) \enspace .
\end{aligned}
$$

Using the definition of $\sigma(\mathcal{C}_x)$ and $y \geq 1$ we see that

$$
I^{<x} < \sum_{y<x} \frac{\Delta^{\alpha/2^y}}{\beta m \cdot \Delta^{0.5 + 1/2^x}} \leq \frac{x-1}{\beta m \cdot \Delta^{\alpha/2^x}} \enspace .
$$

4.2 Competitive Ratios below Δ^d

For the total interference we use $x \geq 1$ and bound as follows

$$\begin{aligned}
I &< \sum_{y \geq x} 2\Delta^{\alpha/2^y} \cdot \left(\frac{3d}{\sigma(\mathcal{C}_y)}\right)^\alpha \cdot \frac{6^d}{\alpha - d} + \frac{x-1}{\beta m \cdot \Delta^{\alpha/2^x}} \\
&\leq \frac{m - x + 1}{\beta m \cdot \Delta^{\alpha/2}} + \frac{x-1}{\beta m \cdot \Delta^{\alpha/2^x}} \\
&\leq \frac{1}{\beta \cdot \Delta^{\alpha/2^x}} \cdot
\end{aligned}$$

As request i is in class $\mathcal{C}_x$, the minimum signal strength is $p_i/d(u_i, v_i)^\alpha \geq 1/\Delta^{\alpha/2^x} > \beta I$, which proves correctness of the algorithm.

For bounding the competitive ratio we again consider the number of requests from the optimum solution that are blocked per accepted request. We consider blocked requests from each class separately. Obviously, the largest blocked areas are generated by a request from class 1. It blocks a hypershpere of radius $\sigma(\mathcal{C}_x)$ for requests from class $\mathcal{C}_x$, which we overestimate by the corresponding sector of side-length $2\sigma(\mathcal{C}_x)$. We must take into account that requests from class $\mathcal{C}_x$ are bounded from below in distance. The proof of the density lemma can be adjusted to show that there can be only $(d+1)^\alpha/\beta$ many receivers and senders in a sector of side-length h when each request has distance at least $d(u_i, v_i) \geq h$. There are only $(d+1)^\alpha (x/h)^d/\beta$ many requests of minimum length h in a sector of side-length x. In the blocked area of $\mathcal{C}_x$ we can schedule at most

$$\frac{(d+1)^\alpha \left(\frac{2\sigma(\mathcal{C}_x)}{\Delta^{1/2^x}}\right)^d}{\beta}$$

many requests. Assuming that d, α, and β are constants, this number is in $\mathcal{O}(m\Delta^{d/2})$ for each $x = 1, \ldots, m-1$. For class $\mathcal{C}_m$ it is in $\mathcal{O}(m\Delta^{d/2 + d/2^m})$. Hence, the total number of requests blocked per accepted request is bounded by $\mathcal{O}(m^2 \Delta^{d/2 + d/2^m})$. In order to obtain a bound for a constant ε, we apply MULTI-CLASS SAFE-DISTANCE using $m = \log d/\varepsilon$ length classes. This proves the theorem. □

4.2.2 Multiple Channels

In this section we show how to generalize the algorithms above to k channels and decrease their competitive ratio. We propose a *k-channel adjustment*,

4. Online Request Scheduling

in which we separate the problem by using certain channels only for specific request lengths. All requests with length in $[\Delta^{(i-1)/k}, \Delta^{i/k}]$ are assigned to channel i, for $i = 1, \ldots, k$, where we assign requests of length $\Delta^{i/k}$ arbitrarily to channel i or $i+1$. For each channel i we apply an algorithm outlined above, which makes decisions about acceptance and power of requests assigned to channel i. Using this separation, we effectively reduce the aspect ratio to $\Delta^{1/k}$ on each channel. If the optimum solution has to adhere to the same length separation on the channels, this would yield a denominator k in the exponents of Δ of the competitive ratios. Obviously, the optimum solution is not tied to our separation, but the possible improvement due to this degree of freedom can easily be bounded by a factor k. This yields the following corollary.

Corollary 4.2.2. MULTI-CLASS SAFE-DISTANCE *with k-channel adjustment is* $\mathcal{O}\left(k\Delta^{(d/2k)+\varepsilon}\right)$-*competitive for the square root power assignment.* SAFE-DISTANCE *with k-channel adjustment is* $\mathcal{O}\left(k\Delta^{d/k}\right)$-*competitive for any polynomial power assignment with $r \in [0,1]$, and* $\mathcal{O}\left(k\Delta^{\max\{r, 1-r\} \cdot d/k}\right)$-*competitive for $r \notin [0,1]$.*

4.2.3 A Randomized Algorithm

In the previous section for $k = \Theta(\log \Delta)$, the length differences on each channel reduce to a constant factor, e.g., for suitable k the requests on channel j are of length $[2^{j-1}, 2^j)$. This implies that we approximate the requests on each channel by a constant factor. Thus, we obtain an $\mathcal{O}(\log \Delta)$-competitive algorithm against an optimum that can use $k = \Theta(\log \Delta)$ channels. Similarly, if the optimum was restricted to use only one channel, we would obtain a constant factor approximation algorithm. This is the main insight for designing our randomized algorithm RANDOM SAFE-DISTANCE.

We virtually set up $\Theta(\log \Delta)$ channels, pick one channel uniformly at random, and then run our algorithm restricted to this channel. This yields an $\mathcal{O}(\log \Delta)$-competitive randomized algorithm, even for the case of a single channel. Using an additional k-channel adjustment in this case shows a similar result for k channels. We have the following corollary.

Corollary 4.2.3. RANDOM SAFE-DISTANCE *with k-channel adjustment is* $\mathcal{O}(\log \Delta)$-*competitive for any polynomial power assignment and any number k of channels.*

4.3 Extensions

Algorithm 6 RANDOM SAFE-DISTANCE
1: Initialize accepted requests $S = \emptyset$.
2: I.u.r. choose $c \in \{1, 2, \ldots, k\}$.
3: **while** a new request i arrives **do**
4:    **if** $d(u_i, v_i) \notin [2^{c-1}, 2^c)$ **then**
5:       decline request: $S' \leftarrow S$.
6:    **else**
7:       Set $p_i = \phi(d_{ii})$ and temporarily accept $S' \leftarrow S \cup i$
8:       **for** all $j \in S$ **do**
9:          **if** $\min\{d(u_i, v_j), d(u_j, v_i)\} \leq \sigma$ **then**
10:            decline request: $S' \leftarrow S$.
11:          **end if**
12:       **end for**
13:    **end if**
14:    Update: $S \leftarrow S'$.
15: **end while**

Note that for polynomial assignments with $r \notin (0, 1)$ and one channel the logarithmic ratio is asymptotically optimal. This follows with a simple example from the previous chapter. There are $n = \Theta(\log \Delta)$ nested request pairs on the line with exponentially increasing distance. The optimum power assignment can successfully schedule $\Omega(\log \Delta)$ requests. Using any polynomial assignment with $r \notin (0, 1)$ there can be only $\mathcal{O}(1)$ successful requests. Thus, using such a power assignment even an optimal offline algorithm knowing all requests is $\Omega(\log \Delta)$-competitive. A similar observation holds with results of [FKRV09] in the case of directed request sets and any distance-based power assignment. In this case, however, the lower bound is only $\Omega(\log \log \Delta)$. Closing this gap remains as an open problem.

4.3 Extensions

4.3.1 Requests with Duration

In the previous sections we assumed that requests last forever, analyzing only the spatial aspect of the problem. We now show how our results extend when each request i has a duration t_i. After time t_i an accepted request stops sending and leaves (thus, no longer causing interference). For simplicity

4. Online Request Scheduling

requests are assumed to arrive in ordered starting time. The extension to arbitrary starting and ending times is straightforward and changes the results by at most a constant factor.

We first show the modification for the algorithm SAFE-DISTANCE for $r \in [0, 1]$. Whenever a request arrives, SAFE-DISTANCE accepts this request iff the safe distance σ to all previous accepted and still sending requests holds. Observe that the optimal solution accepts at most $\mathcal{O}(\Delta^d)$ requests, when SAFE-DISTANCE accepts a request i with $t_i = 1$. Request i blocks only requests that start while i sends, and each blocked request has length at least t_i. This reduces the analysis to spatial aspects. Furthermore, a request i with $t_i = \Gamma$ can be split into Γ requests of length 1, thus blocking at most $\mathcal{O}(\Gamma \cdot \Delta^d)$ requests. The argumentation is similar for other polynomial power assignments and results in an additional factor of Γ in all previously shown bounds (cf. Section 1.3.3).

In the case of multiple channels, for $k = k' \cdot k''$, clustering of requests w.r.t. similar length and duration values can be used to improve the ratio for MULTI-CLASS SAFE-DISTANCE to $\mathcal{O}\left(k \cdot \Gamma^{1/k'} \Delta^{(d/2k'') + \varepsilon}\right)$. Choosing $k = \log \Gamma \cdot \log \Delta$, RANDOM SAFE-DISTANCE becomes $\mathcal{O}\left(\log \Gamma \cdot \log \Delta\right)$-competitive.

4.3.2 Doubling Metrics

All of our algorithms can be adjusted to work in more generalized metric spaces. In particular, we consider doubling metrics [Cla06]. Let $(\mathcal{V}, d)$ be a metric space and $B(x, r) = \{y \in \mathcal{V} \mid d(x, y) \leq r\}$ a *ball* of radius r around a point x. Consider an ϵ-*covering* of such a ball, i.e., a set of balls of radius ϵr such that their union contains $B(x, r)$. The *doubling dimension* of a metric space is the minimum number d such that for any ball $B(x, 2r)$ with $x \in \mathcal{V}$ and $r > 0$ there is a covering with 2^d balls of radius r. A metric with constant d is called a *doubling metric*. We again assume that α and d are constants, and that we have a fading metric with $\alpha > d$. A slight adjustment of the constants involved in the definition of the safe distance then yields similar bounds on the performance of SAFE-DISTANCE, MULTI-CLASS SAFE-DISTANCE, and RANDOM SAFE-DISTANCE in this more general scenario.

Theorem 4.3.1. *All bounds on the competitive ratios of* SAFE-DISTANCE, MULTI-CLASS SAFE-DISTANCE, *and* RANDOM SAFE-DISTANCE *continue to*

4.3 Extensions

hold for doubling fading metrics. In particular, for $k = k' \cdot k''$, MULTI-CLASS SAFE-DISTANCE with k-channel adjustment is $\mathcal{O}\left(k \cdot \Gamma^{1/k'} \cdot \Delta^{(d/2k'')+\varepsilon}\right)$-competitive for the square root power assignment. RANDOM SAFE-DISTANCE with k-channel adjustment is $\mathcal{O}(\log \Gamma \cdot \log \Delta)$-competitive for any polynomial power assignment and any number k of channels.

Proof. **Algorithm SAFE-DISTANCE:** Let us first consider an adjusted algorithm SAFE-DISTANCE that uses the uniform power assignment and keeps a distance of at least

$$\tau = \max\left\{2\Delta, \Delta \cdot 20 \cdot \sqrt[\alpha]{\frac{2\beta}{2^\alpha - 2^d}}\right\}.$$

Then no two senders can be closer than $\tau/2$. Thus, in a ball of radius $\tau/5$ there can be at most two senders. We first require correctness of the algorithm and derive a lower bound on τ. We structure the space into balls of radius $2^\ell \cdot \tau/5$, for $\ell = 1, 2, \ldots$. A ball of size ℓ can be covered by at most 2^d many balls of layer $\ell - 1$. Applying this argument recursively, the ball can be covered by $2^{\ell d}$ of radius $\tau/10$. Note that there can be at most $2^{\ell d+1}$ many different senders in such a ball, because the number of balls of radius r required for covering is at most the number of points with mutual distance $2r$ that can be placed in an area. We now overestimate the number of senders and at a distance by using concentric balls around a receiver v_i. We consider an annulus $B(v_i, 2^\ell \cdot \tau/5) - B(v_i, 2^{\ell-1} \cdot \tau/5)$, and assume that $2^{\ell d+1}$ senders are located in this area, which all have a distance of $2^{\ell-1} \cdot \tau/5$ to v_i. As there is a minimum distance of τ of any sender to v_i, we start to count at $\ell = 2$. This yields an upper bound for the interference of

$$\begin{aligned}
I &< \sum_{\ell=2}^{\infty} \frac{2^{(l+1)d+1}}{(2^\ell \cdot \tau/5)^\alpha} \\
&= 2^{d+1} \cdot \left(\frac{5}{\tau}\right)^\alpha \cdot \sum_{\ell=2}^{\infty} (2^{d-\alpha})^\ell \\
&< 2^{d+1} \cdot \left(\frac{5}{\tau}\right)^\alpha \cdot \left(\frac{2^\alpha}{2^\alpha - 2^d}\right).
\end{aligned} \quad (4.4)$$

For the last inequality we have used that $\alpha > d$. This yields $2^{d-\alpha} < 1$,

4. Online Request Scheduling

and the sum amounts to less than $1/(1-2^{d-\alpha})$. This allows to derive a lower bound of τ on our safe distance, which is satisfied by our choice, and proves correctness.

For bounding the competitive ratio we adjust the Density Lemma in a straightforward way and note that in a ball of radius 1 there can be only $3^\alpha/\beta$ many senders and receivers. To cover a ball of radius τ, we need at most $2^{\lceil \log_2 \tau \rceil d}$ many balls of radius 1. Thus, for α, β and d being constants, there are at most $\mathcal{O}\left(\Delta^d\right)$ many requests that are blocked in the optimum by any accepted request of the online algorithm.

Note that the previous proof can be generalized easily to any polynomial power assignment, resulting in similar bounds as shown in Corollary 4.1.4.

Algorithm MULTI-CLASS SAFE-DISTANCE: For algorithm MULTI-CLASS SAFE-DISTANCE we use the same distribution of request lengths into classes $\mathcal{C}_x$ for $x = 1, \ldots, m$ as before. The safe distances $\tau(\mathcal{C}_x)$ used by the algorithm can be estimated similarly. In particular, we use

$$\tau(\mathcal{C}_x) = \max\left\{2\Delta^{a_{x-1}}, \Delta^{0.5+a_x} \cdot 20 \cdot \sqrt[\alpha]{2\beta m \cdot \left(2 + \frac{1}{2^\alpha - 2^d}\right)}\right\}.$$

The construction to show correctness is the same extension that we used to extend SAFE-DISTANCE to MULTI-CLASS SAFE-DISTANCE as before. Here, however, we use the bounds of Equation 4.4, which yields

$$I < \sum_{y \geq x} 2\Delta^{\alpha/2^y} \cdot \left(\frac{20}{\tau(\mathcal{C}_y)}\right)^\alpha \cdot \frac{1}{2^\alpha - 2^d} + \underbrace{\sum_{y<x} \Delta^{\alpha/2^y} \sum_{j \in \mathcal{C}_y} \frac{1}{d(u_j, v_i)^\alpha}}_{I^{<x}}.$$

Using a minimum distance of $\tau(\mathcal{C}_x)$ for the requests from the smallest balls, we derive similarly as before

$$\begin{aligned} I^{<x} &\leq 2\sum_{y<x} \Delta^{\alpha/2^y} \cdot \left(\frac{2^d}{\tau(\mathcal{C}_x)^\alpha} + \left(\frac{5}{\tau(\mathcal{C}_y)}\right)^\alpha \cdot \left(4^d + \sum_{\ell=2}^\infty \frac{2^{(\ell+1)d}}{2^{\ell\alpha}}\right)\right) \\ &< \sum_{y<x} 2\Delta^{\alpha/2^y} \cdot \left(\frac{2^d}{\tau(\mathcal{C}_x)^\alpha} + \left(\frac{5}{\tau(\mathcal{C}_y)}\right)^\alpha \cdot \left(4^d + \frac{2^{\alpha+d}}{2^\alpha - 2^d}\right)\right) \end{aligned}$$

4.3 Extensions

$$\leq \sum_{y<x} 2\Delta^{\alpha/2^y} \cdot \left(\frac{20}{\tau(\mathcal{C}_x)}\right)^\alpha \cdot \left(2 + \frac{1}{2^\alpha - 2^d}\right) .$$

Thus, by using the definition of $\tau(\mathcal{C}_x)$ and noting $y \geq 1$ we see that $I^{<x} < \frac{x-1}{\beta m \cdot \Delta^{\alpha/2^x}}$. For the total interference we use $x \geq 1$ and bound as follows

$$I < \sum_{y \geq x} 2\Delta^{\alpha/2^y} \cdot \left(\frac{20}{\tau(\mathcal{C}_y)}\right)^\alpha \cdot \frac{1}{2^\alpha - 2^d} + \frac{x-1}{\beta m \cdot \Delta^{\alpha/2^x}} \leq \frac{1}{\beta \cdot \Delta^{\alpha/2^x}} ,$$

which proves correctness of the algorithm. Estimation of the competitive ratio can be done similarly as before. We use the adjustment of the Density Lemma outlined above for SAFE-DISTANCE to bound the maximum number of connections from OPT blocked by MULTI-CLASS SAFE-DISTANCE. This results in a competitive ratio of $\mathcal{O}\left(\Delta^{(d/2)+\varepsilon}\right)$.

Channels and RANDOM SAFE-DISTANCE: The generalization to multiple channels and the randomized algorithm are independent of the metric and apply directly without adjustment.

□

4. Online Request Scheduling

Chapter 5
Conclusions

Recently, scientists start to understand the power and limitations of wireless networks. This thesis is part of this process with the following contributions for scheduling problems in the physical model.

We focus on applying oblivious power schemes as transmission power, that is, the power for a signal is defined as a function of the path loss. The major advantage of these power assignments is their simplicity. In particular, they can be locally computed for every request without taking into account other requests. The most common examples of such power assignments are the uniform, the linear and the square root power assignment. We present several approximation algorithms as well as lower bounds for scheduling in the unidirectional and bidirectional setting and initiate the research of online capacity maximization.

In the first part of this thesis we analyze scheduling using the linear power assignment. This assignment is of special interest as it is energy efficient in the sense that signals are sent at a power level that is only a constant factor larger than the power level needed to drown out ambient noise. The key to both the lower and upper bounds is the measure of interference I. On the one hand, we show that $\Omega(I)$ is a lower bound on the schedule length when using linear power assignments. On the other hand, we present distributed scheduling algorithms for the linear power assignment computing schedules of length $\mathcal{O}(I \log n)$ and $\mathcal{O}(I + \log^2 n)$, respectively. For dense instances this yields a constant-factor approximation to the optimal schedule for linear power assignment. To the best of our knowledge, our result is so far the only constant-factor approximation algorithm for the scheduling problem in the physical model.

5. Conclusions

For the capacity maximization problem, that is, selecting a maximal subset of feasible requests, there are constant-factor approximations known not only for uniform power assignments [GHWW09], but recently even for all length-monotone sublinear power assignments [HM10]. These results directly imply logarithmic approximation factors for scheduling. It still remains an open question if these results can be improved to get rid of the logarithmic factor.

How do these results compare to the schedule length for general power assignments? For the linear power assignment we show a lower bound of $\Omega(I/\log \Delta \log n)$ for schedules with general power assignments, where Δ denotes the aspect ratio of the metric. When restricting to the two-dimensional Euclidean space the bound improves to $\Omega(I/\log \Delta)$. A similar result for uniform power is a direct consequence from [AD09]. Thus, the best known scheduling algorithms for the linear and the uniform power assignments achieve approximation ratios of order $\log \Delta \cdot \text{polylog } n$ in comparison to the optimal power assignment.

It turns out that the dependence on the aspect ratio Δ is unavoidable for nontrivial results. For each oblivious power assignment we present a family of instances that, on the one hand needs $\Omega(n)$ steps for this oblivious power assignment, on the other hand can be scheduled in a constant number of rounds with different power – this corresponds to the worst possible performance guarantee.

The situation changes significantly when considering bidirectional communication. Although the negative results for the uniform and linear power assignment hold in the bidirectional setting, this is not true for all oblivious power assignments. Introducing the technique of decomposing requests from general metric spaces to easier understandable star metrics, we prove that the square root power assignment yields polylogarithmic schedules in the bidirectional setting. This result triggered the interest in the square root assignment and was further improved by Halldórsson to a $\log n$ approximation [Hal09, HM10]. In fact, Halldórssons work underlined the importance of the square root assignment, as it turned out that this assignment is essentially the best possible for bidirectional scheduling.

Solutions for bidirectional scheduling are fixed to assign the same power to both endpoints of a request. We consider oblivious power assignments which fulfill this restriction by definition. It would be interesting to see, if breaking up this symmetry by either assigning different powers or time slots to the endpoints of a pair could substantially outperform the known algorithms.

In the last part, we consider the capacity maximization problem under the assumption that an algorithm does not know in advance when requests arrive. On arrival it must be decided if to accept or reject the presented request. We present an optimal deterministic online algorithms for this problem and show that their bounds can significantly be beaten by a simple randomized algorithm. Still, there is a remarkable gap between the performance of deterministic offline and online algorithms. This gap is caused by the fact that most offline algorithms somehow process the requests by distance, which is clearly not possible here. Finding better randomized online algorithms or a matching lower bound will answer the question if this gap can be closed by using randomization.

We are aware that the physical model – although more realistic than graph based models – is a simplification of real world scenarios. It remains a challenging problem whether the results for scheduling hold in more realistic interference models like Rayleigh or Rician fading models.

5. Conclusions

Bibliography

[AD09] Matthew Andrews and Michael Dinitz. Maximizing capacity in arbitrary wireless networks in the SINR model: Complexity and game theory. In *Proceedings of the 28th Conference of the IEEE Communications Society (INFOCOM)*, 2009.

[adHV95] Friedhelm Meyer auf der Heide and Berthold Vöcking. A packet routing protocol for arbitrary networks. In *Proceedings of the 12th International Symposium on Theoretical Aspects of Computer Science (STACS)*, pages 291–302, 1995.

[AEK$^+$09] Chen Avin, Yuval Emek, Erez Kantor, Zvi Lotker, David Peleg, and Liam Roditty. SINR diagrams: towards algorithmically usable SINR models of wireless networks. In *Proceedings of the 28th Annual ACM Symposium on Principles of Distributed Computing (PODC)*, pages 200–209, New York, NY, USA, 2009. ACM.

[ALP09] Chen Avin, Zvi Lotker, and Yvonne Anne Pignolet. On the power of uniform power: Capacity of wireless networks with bounded resources. In *Proceedings of the 17th Annual European Symposium on Algorithms (ESA)*, 2009.

[ALPP09] Chen Avin, Zvi Lotker, Francesco Pasquale, and Yvonne Anne Pignolet. A note on uniform power connectivity in the SINR model. In *Proceedings of the 5th International Workshop on Algorithmic Aspects of Wireless Sensor Networks (ALGOSENSORS)*, pages 116–127, 2009.

Bibliography

[BL03] Nikhil Bansal and Zhen Liu. Capacity, delay and mobility in wireless ad-hoc networks. *Conference of the IEEE Communications Society (INFOCOM)*, 2:1553–1563, 2003.

[BM02] Suman Banerjee and Archan Misra. Minimum energy paths for reliable communication in multi-hop wireless networks. In *Proceedings of the 3rd ACM International Symposium Mobile Ad-Hoc Networking and Computing (MOBIHOC)*, pages 146–156, 2002.

[CKM+07] Deepti Chafekar, V. S. Anil Kumar, Madhav V. Marathe, Srinivasan Parthasarathy, and Aravind Srinivasan. Cross-layer latency minimization in wireless networks with SINR constraints. In *Proceedings of the 8th ACM International Symposium Mobile Ad-Hoc Networking and Computing (MOBIHOC)*, pages 110–119, 2007.

[CKM+08] Deepti Chafekar, V. S. Anil Kumar, Madhav V. Marathe, Srinivasan Parthasarathy, and Aravind Srinivasan. Approximation algorithms for computing capacity of wireless networks with SINR constraints. In *Proceedings of the 27th Conference of the IEEE Communications Society (INFOCOM)*, pages 1166–1174, 2008.

[Cla06] Kenneth L. Clarkson. Nearest-neighbor searching and metric space dimensions. In G. Shakhnarovich, T. Darell, and P. Indyk, editors, *Nearest-Neighbor Methods for Learning and Vision: Theory and Practice*, pages 15–59. MIT Press, 2006.

[Din10] Michael Dinitz. Distributed algorithms for approximating wireless network capacity. In *Proceedings of the 29th Conference of the IEEE Communications Society (INFOCOM)*, pages 1397–1405, Piscataway, NJ, USA, 2010. IEEE Press.

[DR98] Devdatt P. Dubhashi and Desh Ranjan. Balls and bins: A study in negative dependence. *Random Structures and Algorithms*, 13(2):99–124, 1998.

Bibliography

[EE04] Tamer A. ElBatt and Anthony Ephremides. Joint scheduling and power control for wireless ad hoc networks. *IEEE Transactions on Wireless Communications*, 3(1):74–85, 2004.

[FGHV10] Alexander Fanghänel, Sascha Geulen, Martin Hoefer, and Berthold Vöcking. Online capacity maximization in wireless networks. In *Proceedings of the 22nd Annual ACM Symposium on Parallel Algorithms and Architectures (SPAA)*, pages 92–99, 2010.

[FKRV09] Alexander Fanghänel, Thomas Kesselheim, Harald Räcke, and Berthold Vöcking. Oblivious interference scheduling. In *Proceedings of the 28th Annual ACM Symposium on Principles of Distributed Computing (PODC)*, pages 220–229, 2009.

[FKV09] Alexander Fanghänel, Thomas Kesselheim, and Berthold Vöcking. Improved algorithms for latency minimization in wireless networks. In *Proceedings of the 36th International EATCS Colloquium on Automata, Languages and Programming (ICALP)*, pages 447–458, 2009.

[GH01] Jimmi Grönkvist and Anders Hansson. Comparison between graph-based and interference-based STDMA scheduling. In *Proceedings of the 2nd ACM International Symposium Mobile Ad-Hoc Networking and Computing (MOBIHOC)*, pages 255–258, 2001.

[GHR06] Anupam Gupta, Mohammad Taghi Hajiaghayi, and Harald Räcke. Oblivious network design. In *Proceedings of the 17th Annual ACM–SIAM Symposium on Discrete Algorithms (SODA)*, pages 970–979, 2006.

[GHWW09] Olga Goussevskaia, Magnús M. Halldórsson, Roger Wattenhofer, and Emo Welzl. Capacity of arbitrary wireless networks. In *Proceedings of the 28th Conference of the IEEE Communications Society (INFOCOM)*, 2009.

[GK98] Piyush Gupta and P. R. Kumar. Critical power for asymptotic connectivity in wireless networks. In William M. McEneaney,

Bibliography

George Yin, and Qing Zhang, editors, *Stochastic Analysis, Control, Optimization, and Applications: A Volume in Honor of W. H. Fleming*, Systems & Control: Foundations & Applications, pages 547–566. Birkhäuser, 1998.

[GK00] Piyush Gupta and P. R. Kumar. The capacity of wireless networks. *IEEE Trans. Information Theory*, 46:388–404, 2000.

[GMW08] Olga Goussevskaia, Thomas Moscibroda, and Roger Wattenhofer. Local broadcasting in the physical interference model. In *Proceedings of the 5th ACM SIGACT/SIGMOBILE International Workshop on Foundations of Mobile Computing (DIALM-POMC)*, pages 35–44, New York, NY, USA, 2008.

[Gou09] Olga Goussevskaia. *Computational Complexity and Scheduling Algorithms for Wireless Networks*. PhD thesis, ETH Zurich, July 2009.

[GOW07] Olga Goussevskaia, Yvonne Anne Oswald, and Roger Wattenhofer. Complexity in geometric SINR. In *Proceedings of the 8th ACM International Symposium Mobile Ad-Hoc Networking and Computing (MOBIHOC)*, pages 100–109, 2007.

[Hal09] Magnús M. Halldórsson. Wireless scheduling with power control. In *Proceedings of the 17th Annual European Symposium on Algorithms (ESA)*, 2009.

[HM04] Ramin Hekmat and Piet Van Mieghem. Interference in wireless multi-hop ad-hoc networks and its effect on network capacity. *Wireless Networks*, 10(4):389–399, 2004.

[HM10] Magnús M. Halldórsson and Pradipta Mitra. Wireless capacity with oblivious power in general metrics. Unpublished manuscript, 2010.

[HW09] Magnús M. Halldórsson and Roger Wattenhofer. Wireless communication is in APX. In *Proceedings of the 36th International EATCS Colloquium on Automata, Languages and Programming (ICALP)*, 2009.

Bibliography

[Kes10] Thomas Kesselheim. A constant-factor approximation for wireless capacity maximization with power control in the SINR model. *CoRR*, abs/1007.1611, 2010.

[KR10] Dariusz Kowalski and Mariusz Rokicki. Connectivity problem in wireless networks. In *Proceedings of the 24th International Symposium on Distributed Computing (DISC)*, volume 6343 of *Lecture Notes in Computer Science*, pages 344–358. Springer Berlin / Heidelberg, 2010.

[KT03] Ulas C. Kozat and Leandros Tassiulas. Network layer support for service discovery in mobile ad hoc networks. In *Proceedings of the 22nd Conference of the IEEE Communications Society (INFOCOM)*, pages 1965–1975, 2003.

[KV10] Thomas Kesselheim and Berthold Vöcking. Distributed contention resolution in wireless networks. In *International Symposium on Distributed Computing (DISC)*, 2010.

[LL09] Emmanuelle Lebhar and Zvi Lotker. Unit disk graph and physical interference model: Putting pieces together. In *Proceedings of the 23rd IEEE International Parallel and Distributed Processing Symposium (IPDPS)*, pages 1–8, 2009.

[LMR94] F. T. Leighton, Bruce M. Maggs, and Satish B. Rao. Packet routing and job-shop scheduling in O(congestion+dilation) steps. *Combinatorica*, 1994.

[LMRR94] F. T. Leighton, Bruce M. Maggs, Abhiram G. Ranade, and Satish B. Rao. Randomized routing and sorting on fixed-connection networks. *Journal of Algorithms*, 1994.

[LP10] Zvi Lotker and David Peleg. Structure and algorithms in the SINR wireless model. *SIGACT News*, 41(2):74–84, 2010.

[MJD08] Ritesh Maheshwari, Shweta Jain, and Samir R. Das. A measurement study of interference modeling and scheduling in low-power wireless networks. In *Proceedings of the 6th International Conference on Embedded Networked Sensor Systems (SenSys)*, pages 141–154, 2008.

Bibliography

[Mos07] Thomas Moscibroda. The worst-case capacity of wireless sensor networks. In *Proceedings of the 6th International Conference on Information Processing in Sensor Networks (IPSN)*, pages 1–10, 2007.

[MOW07] Thomas Moscibroda, Yvonne Anne Oswald, and Roger Wattenhofer. How optimal are wireless scheduling protocols? In *Proceedings of the 26th Conference of the IEEE Communications Society (INFOCOM)*, pages 1433–1441, 2007.

[MW06] Thomas Moscibroda and Roger Wattenhofer. The complexity of connectivity in wireless networks. In *Proceedings of the 25th Conference of the IEEE Communications Society (INFOCOM)*, pages 1–13, 2006.

[MWW06] Thomas Moscibroda, Roger Wattenhofer, and Yves Weber. Protocol Design Beyond Graph-Based Models. In *Proceedings of the 5th Workshop on Hot Topics in Networks (HotNets)*, 2006.

[MWZ06] Thomas Moscibroda, Roger Wattenhofer, and Aaron Zollinger. Topology control meets SINR: The scheduling complexity of arbitrary topologies. In *Proceedings of the 7th ACM International Symposium Mobile Ad-Hoc Networking and Computing (MOBIHOC)*, pages 310–321, 2006.

[Rag88] Prabhakar Raghavan. Probabilistic construction of deterministic algorithms: Approximating packing integer programs. *Journal of Computer and System Sciences*, 37(2):130–143, 1988.

[Rap01] Theodore S. Rappaport. *Wireless Communications: Principles and Practice*. Prentice Hall PTR, Upper Saddle River, NJ, USA, 2001.

[RT87] Prabhakar Raghavan and Clark D. Tompson. Randomized rounding: A technique for provably good algorithms and algorithmic proofs. *Combinatorica*, 7(4):365–374, 1987.

[SR98] Suresh Singh and C. S. Raghavendra. PAMAS—Power aware multi-access protocol with signalling for ad hoc networks. *ACM SIGCOMM Computer Communication Review*, 28(3):5–26, 1998.

Bibliography

[ST97]   Aravind Srinivasan and Chung-Piaw Teo. A constant-factor approximation algorithm for packet routing, and balancing local vs. global criteria. In *Proceedings of the 29th Annual ACM Symposium on Theory of Computing (STOC)*, pages 636–643, New York, NY, USA, 1997.

[WNE02] Jeffrey Wieselthier, Gam Nguyen, and Anthony Ephremides. Energy-efficient broadcast and multicast trees in wireless networks. *Mobile Networks and Applications (MONET)*, 7(6):481–492, 2002.

Bibliography

Die VDM Verlagsservicegesellschaft sucht für wissenschaftliche Verlage abgeschlossene und herausragende

Dissertationen, Habilitationen, Diplomarbeiten, Master Theses, Magisterarbeiten usw.

für die kostenlose Publikation als Fachbuch.

Sie verfügen über eine Arbeit, die hohen inhaltlichen und formalen Ansprüchen genügt, und haben Interesse an einer honorarvergüteten Publikation?

Dann senden Sie bitte erste Informationen über sich und Ihre Arbeit per Email an *info@vdm-vsg.de*.

Sie erhalten kurzfristig unser Feedback!

VDM Verlagsservicegesellschaft mbH
Dudweiler Landstr. 99   Telefon +49 681 3720 174
D - 66123 Saarbrücken   Fax   +49 681 3720 1749

www.vdm-vsg.de

Die VDM Verlagsservicegesellschaft mbH vertritt

Printed by Books on Demand GmbH, Norderstedt / Germany